MIND CONTROL

The book set include

1) DARK PSYCHOLOGY

2) ANALYZE PEOPLE

TABLE OF CONTENTS

DARK PSYCHOLOGY

TABLE OF CONTENTS

ANALYZE PEOPLE

DARK

PSYCHOLOGY

The Art and Science of Manipulation and Mind
Control. The Secrets and Tactics That People
Use for Motivation, Persuasion, Manipulation
and
Coercion to Get What They Want.

© Text Copyright 2019 – Jason Halpa

implied. Readers acknowledge that the author is not engaging in the rendering of legal, financial, medical or professional advice. The content within this book has been derived from various sources. Please consult a licensed professional before attempting any techniques outlined in this book.

By reading this document, the reader agrees that under no circumstances is the author responsible for any losses, direct or indirect, which are incurred as a result of the use of information contained within this document, including, but not limited to, — errors, omissions, or inaccuracies.

INTRODUCTION

The knowledge of dark psychology presented in this book is not intended to be used to cause harm to others. Rather, the main objective is to help you recognize manipulation in its various forms for what it is and if need be, to turn the tables to protect yourself. If you can manipulate a manipulator before they get the best of you, then that is a win for you and the rest of humanity.

You are probably confused by this one because you have always believed that smarter people are harder to outwit, right? Here's the thing though: intelligent people like to use logic to aid their decision-making process. Logic is easier to manipulate. Hence, intelligent people are more likely to manipulated when you corner them with logical arguments. Less intelligent people are harder to convince with logic and tend to be more stubborn in the face of facts and scientific arguments. It is no wonder that a whole lot of people who have been scammed by con artists and Ponzi schemes happen to be people who are relatively smart and who you'd not expect to be easily fooled. The reason why this is often the case is because scammers know to appeal to this kind of people with facts and statistics. People who are less smart will be easily dismissive of anything that sounds like hullabaloo because they do not understand it.

You are trusting and like to believe the best about everyone

Believe it or not, there are bad people in this world. There are people who leave their homes every morning with the intention of harming others. There are people who have no qualms about inflicting heartache and turmoil upon others. While you may be seated in your house worrying about mega rich corporations who steal from the poor, there is a boardroom full of corporate big shots who are about to steal from the very poor that you are worried about. Simply put, not everybody shares in your conscience and your empathy. People are wired differently. People on the dark triad are wired even more different than you could ever imagine. When you meet a new person, it is noble to want to believe the best of them, but it is wise to expect to be surprised in a not-so-great way. Keeping your expectations of people to a minimum is a great way to protect yourself against everyone that is trying to get a piece of you.

WHAT IS DARK PSYCHOLOGY?

Most psychological techniques have a dual purpose – they can be used for both dark psychology and white psychology. What differs is the intent of the person employing the techniques.

In this chapter, we will concern ourselves with psychological techniques employed to achieve nefarious intents.

Dark persuasion

Persuasion is by far the most employed psychological technique. Most of the time, it is used for White psychology. As a tool for White psychology, almost all of us have used it in one way or another. However, very few of us have employed persuasion as a dark psychology tool.

Before we venture into the depth of Dark persuasion, let's look at the crucial components of persuasion as a whole.

What is persuasion?

Persuasion is a psychological technique of presenting arguments in such a way that motivates, influences, or changes a person's attitude, or behavior in order to achieve the desired outcome.

Persuasion tips

The following are important tips you need to master in order to become successfully persuasive:

- Do your research – to gain knowledgeable authoritative

- Be a thought leader – to guide people in your thoughts

- Be confident

- Appeal to emotions

Use rhetoric statements and assertions

- Keep sarcasm to the minimum

- Sound reasonable

- Watch reactions

- Be subtle in responses

- Actively listen

- Suggest, don't demand

- Be actively observant

- Be emotionally intelligent

Persuasion tactics

The following are basic yet important persuasion tactics:

- Use the name of the person you are engaging with

- Make a personal connection

- Build rapport

- Create an opportunity for reciprocity

- Use motivating words

- Be dynamic and adaptive – like a chameleon, change to suit your target's uniqueness (no blanket approach). Use NLP's mirroring and matching technique.

- Take advantage of the Bandwagon effect

- Create some scarcity in the mind of the person you are persuading

- Inspire curiosity through deliberate information gap (suspense)

- Use a foot in the door tactic – make a small request that opens the door wider for an eventual big request

- Clearly, point out the benefit of your proposition to the person you are persuading. Remember everyone subconsciously asks "what is in it for me?"

The Bandwagon effect

Bandwagon effect refers to that effect a crowd or group of people has on its constituent member.

The following are some characteristic attributes of the bandwagon effect:

- The herd mentality – people are persuaded to follow each other

- Social proof - people tend to follow the most popular cause of action. For example, decrying negative social proof (such as littering, logging, bad sexual behavior, bingeing, smoking, etc) may actually promote it. For example, in case of 20% absenteeism, instead of the manager decrying that there is an increase of absenteeism from the previous 15% to now 20%, the manager should also reinforce positive social proof by pointing out to the majority who have remained not absent (i.e. 80%) and talk of the 20% as few spoilt apples that should be minimized.

Deception

Deception refers consciously and deliberately promoting that which is not true with the aim of covering-up, misleading, or promoting a belief, concept or idea with the aim of manipulating the recipient to act or respond in a certain predetermined way.

In other words, deception is manipulation of appearances such that they convey a false reality.

The core essence of deception is to disguise. Some of the common deception methods include:

- Propaganda – propagating false information and packaging it as truth or facts

- Camouflage – disguising the true nature of things. For example, a spy using philanthropy to penetrate a community.

- Pretension – taking a form that is false from the true form. For example pretending to be innocent while guilty, pretending to be sick while well, pretending to grief while inside you are celebrating, etc.

- Mystification – creating a supernatural sense by hoarding truth and acting in a way that appears supernormal. This makes you attractive to those who are prone to beliefs.

- Paltering – speak or act in such a manner that bamboozles people and as such draw their attention away from themselves and towards you. Eventually, you manipulate their attention towards achieving your own set goals. Conjurers, magicians, and actors employ this tactic.

Types of deception

Deception occurs in two primary forms:

- Lie by commission (dissimulation) – this is the active part of the deception. In lie by the commission, a person deceives or lies directly by deliberately altering material facts.

- Lie by omission(simulation) – lie by omission is indirect. In this regard, a person engaged in deception does not deliberately alter material facts. Rather, the person knowingly and deliberately conceals material facts which he or she knows that would have altered the decision of the person being deceived.

Dupery

Dupery is an act of deception. However, dupery goes further to selfishly gain from the victim. In dupery, the manipulator sets traps or baits into which the victim falls in and then gets exploited for selfish or nefarious gains.

Indoctrination

Indoctrination is the act of imparting someone with a

set of beliefs without offering that person an opportunity for critical inquiry.

Indoctrination strategies:

Rote training – this is an act of enforcing information into people's memory through repetitive action. For example, uttering certain mantra during prayers, or counting mala beads while praying.

Affirmation–making people say words that positively approve certain statements. This way, they are programmed to hold those statements as true.

Obstruction of truth and facts–this is a deliberate action aimed at making those being indoctrinated not to access sources of truth or facts. For example, they can be barred from reading certain books that are deemed "satanic". Fear psychology is often employed, like telling people that they will have nightmares or be visited by vampire spirits in their sleep if they read such a book.

Confession–everyone one of us has a "sinful" past. We all have skeletons in our past... things that we did and feel guilty about. One indoctrination strategy is to force people to confess. Once they confess, they lose the moral authority to stand upright before the indoctrinators. As such, they become more submissive toward indoctrination.

Isolation – the main aim of isolation is to cut out someone from the influence that may make indoctrination impossible or difficult to achieve. Thus, the victims are cut off from the rest of the family, society or normal relationships. Isolation is one form of obstruction of truth and facts since the victims cannot get a second opinion about assertions being made by the indoctrinators.

Guilt imposition – guilt imposition is closely related to forced confession. However, in guilt imposition, a sense of guilt is postulated into the victim's mind. The victim may be unknowingly ensnared to commit a wrong and then indoctrinator finds ways to discover it. Later on, the indoctrinator uses that act to impose guilt on the victim. The primary objective, just as forced confession, is to lower the victim's moral standing and hence cower the victim into psychological submission.

Phobia imposition – phobia is psychological fear. Indoctrinators induce phobia into their victims such that they find it hard to exist outside the indoctrinator's domain. For example, the victim can be told of how the 'devil' wants to kill him and the only way to salvation is to leave that devil-infested home and come to live with the indoctrinator who has the powers to chase away the devil. There are many forms of phobia imposition. For example, insurance companies impose phobia on their potential clients by exaggerating the potential risks that may happen should the potential client not insure the life of loved ones or property. Governments also prey on their citizens by instilling phobia, especially when they want their agenda to prevail.

Rituals – rituals have a strong effect on one's psychology. This is why most traditions, religions, cults, political organizations, and even some civil organizations have rituals. For example, it is common for rituals to be performed prior to prayers, prior to burials, prior to the war, etc. Rituals enhance a person susceptibility to a certain proposition being advanced by the indoctrinator.

Induced dependency – induced dependency is commonly applied by manipulators in a relationship where they want to gain an upper hand over their victims. For example, imperialist or colonialist entities can perpetuate poverty in their target society and then pretend to be saviors of that society. They may dish out conditional aid, conditional grant, etc... with the conditions carefully crafted to increase dependency and make the victims more susceptible to exploitation. Since, without this deliberate impoverishment, that particular society would not have become susceptibly poor or would not have welcomed the conditional aid and grant, this becomes and induced dependency. In marriage partners, it is common for an insecure partner to create a condition that makes the other partner dependent. For example, an insecure husband can push or trigger his wife to lose employment. Once the wife loses employment, then, the insecure husband feels comfortably in control of the unemployed wife since he is the main breadwinner. The wife's lack of financial independence makes her become more susceptible to the dictates of the husband.

Punishment – by having a system of tests and exams and offering incentives for those who pass the indoctrination program

Characteristics of indoctrination

Unsurprisingly indoctrination takes place in most domains of our lives. It takes place in our homes (by parents), in schools (by teachers), in public life (by politicians and governments), etc.

The following are some of the key characteristics of tools used for indoctrination:

- Fear
- Dogmatism
- Fundamentalism
- Cognitive closure
- Feeling of inadequacy
- Perceived deprivation

Sources of indoctrination

While there are some covert sources of indoctrination, the following are some of the common overt sources of indoctrination:

- Religious institutions
- Schools and educational establishments
- Media – mainstream, alternative media, social media

- Parents

- Politicians

- Marriage partners

Brainwashing

Brainwashing refers to erasing from one's belief system the existing set of old beliefs and in its place supplanting a new set of beliefs. Brainwashing happens without someone's will.

While sometimes brainwashing is subtle and involuntary, a lot of time it is violent. For example, we've had forced conversions during the crusade period and also during the jihad. In the forced conversion, the victims are fully aware that they are being brainwashed but accept it as a coping mechanism to avoid greater harm such as death.

Violent brainwashing happens most in the militant cultic or criminal organizations where victims are trapped and have no exit option.

Potential victims of violent brainwashing include:

- Prisoners (especially prisoners of war)

- Slaves under captivity

- Kidnapped victims

- Illegal aliens

In the subtle brainwashing, often the victim voluntarily and unknowingly accepts brainwashing. In this case, the perpetrator looks out for susceptible victims who are more malleable. The victims are often in a desperate situation and thus have a psychological void that desires fulfillment.

- The following are some of the potential victims of unknowing brainwashing:

- Those suffering from unknown chronic illness

- Minors who have left their home to live alone and often faraway

- Those who have lost their jobs and are in deep despair

- Those who have lost their loved ones, especially through divorce or death

Common steps in brainwashing

The following are some of the common steps taken by

brainwashers to brainwash their victims:

- Isolation

- Attack on self-esteem

- subjugation

- Testing

- Love bombing

Isolation

The brainwasher knows that a person's family or close circle can easily notice what is happening and thus rescue the victim. As such, the first step they take is to isolate the victim from close family and friends.

Some, like cultic leaders, can instill negativities about close family and friends. This brings division between the victim and loved ones and thus breeds psychological isolation. For example, a cultic leader can claim that your closest friend is a psychic vampire that drains your energy thus making you chronically ill and as such you ought to keep off from that friend. Since you are sick and desperate, you are likely to follow this brainwashing tactic and thus find yourself isolated from the very person who could have saved you from brainwashing.

Attack on self-esteem

It is only a victim who has self-doubt, low self-confidence, and on the overall suffers from low self-esteem that can easily be brainwashed. As such, the brainwasher seeks to achieve this state in the victim by attacking the victim's self-esteem.

Some of the ways by which the brainwasher attacks the victim's self-esteem include:

- Verbal and physical abuse – this often applied in violent brainwashing where the brainwasher uses abuse as a means of demeaning the victim so that the victim loses self-worth.

- Sleep deprivation – a sleep-deprived person is more likely to submit to psychological pressure since there is lack of full consciousness. It is much easier for a sleep-deprived person to submit to brainwashing instructions just to have an opportunity to be left alone and sleep.

- Intimidation–Intimidation is one of the tactics employed by brainwashers to push someone into involuntary submission. For example, the threat of punishment is a form of intimidation.

- Embarrassment – this is used especially if the victim has some dark secret that he or she wouldn't like to be revealed. For example, a brainwasher may resort to using tricks to obtain nude photos of a potential victim or trick such a victim into marital infidelity. Once the brainwasher acquires these materials, he/she starts subtly embarrassing the victim. In this subtle embarrassment, the brainwasher doesn't reveal the materials to the public but uses generalized terms that insinuate immorality on the part of the victim. The victim knows where the cues are leading to and thus does everything possible to dissuade the brainwasher from revealing these embarrassing contents. Thus, the brainwasher attains an upper hand which he/she uses to brainwash the victim. For example, the victim could be forced into performing rituals that wear the victim's self-worth and self-esteem thus becoming deeply captive to the brainwasher. Eventually, the victim may be infected by the Stockholm syndrome, where, instead of acting against the brainwasher, acts to protect the brainwasher – an act, which, subconsciously is more about protecting the "secrets" (embarrassing content).

- Scarcity creation such as rationing of basic necessities and only released upon the victim's obedient performance.

Subjugation

Brainwashers seek to bring the victim under their absolute control so that the victims become absolutely obedient.

The following are some of the tactics used to achieve subjugation:

- Extreme abuse

- Us -vs- Them

- Love bombing

Extreme abuse

The victim is passed through extreme abuse. Almost

often emotional and psychological abuses are employed. Physical abuse is only employed in violent brainwashing. Physical abuse is not employed in the subtle brainwashing.

Us -vs- Them

The victim is coerced to make a choice between the brainwasher and the rest of the world. However, the victim is not granted an exit option.

The victim is introduced to those who are already brainwashed and thus praise the brainwasher. In case the victim still thinks of "them" (the outside world) as an option, the victim continues to be subjected to extreme abuse until he or she comes the ultimate choice of belonging to "us", that is, joining the rest of the brainwashed subjects.

Testing

Testing happens to establish whether the victim has ultimately made the "us' choice and no longer desires to join "them". It is also done to test the victim's level of obedience.

Sometimes, under secret control, the victim may be released to "them" (the rest of the world) on the condition that he or she should return on a certain date. The victim is then secretly monitored to see whether he/she desires to return to "us" (the brainwashed group).

If the victim doesn't desire to return to "us", then, the victim is kidnapped and returned to the fold upon which the vicious cycle begins.

On the other hand, if the victim voluntarily returns to us, then, the victim is taken to the next stage, that is, love bombing.

More often than not, due to isolation and induced dependency, even if the victim desires to rejoin "them", the victim finds it such a long journey to recovery and hence prefers getting back to "us" rather than starting all over again to rebuild the lost life.

Love bombing

Once tests are done and prove that the victim has been effectively brainwashed, love bombing is applied to galvanize the victim into the fold.

Love bombing could be in the form of praising, promotion in the order of subjects, receiving gifts, etc.

Dark Seduction

Dark seduction refers to the use of dark psychological tools to entice someone into engaging in a relationship that satisfies seducer's self-interest with no apparent benefit to the seducee.

A dark seducer orchestrates the victim's longings to suit his/her selfish desires.

While seduction is traditionally related to the opposite sex, it can also be of the same gender and asexual.

Dark seduction is not necessarily about sex but taking advantage of sexual arousal to achieve certain objectives.

When a victim is sexually aroused, the victim becomes less logical and less rational and thus more susceptible to manipulation.

The following are some of the dark seduction techniques:

- Love bombing
- erotic expressions
- platitudes

- gifting

- sexual innuendos

The primary objective of dark seduction is to appeal to the primitive Id within every individual and reduce the effect of anti-cathexis. This makes the victim break away from super-ego and hence lowers to the primitive level of Id where hedonism is prevalent.

Erotic actions and rewards are applied to the victim to reinforce this state of Id and completely wear off the super-ego and anti-cathexis.

More often than not, indoctrination and brainwashing can be applied to facilitate the wearing off of the super-ego.

Hypnotization

Hypnotization is the act of drawing a person's mind to a receptively vulnerable state that is irresistibly open to your suggestions.

A hypnotized person is like a sleep-walker whose consciousness is deeply focused on the act of walking and completely isolated to signals emanating from the rest of the environment.

While in that state of hypnotism, the hypnotized person cannot consciously draw references from external sources but only from the suggestions. The person either largely or completely loses peripheral awareness. Thus, the person's mind is trapped into some sort of a conscious bubble that is impermeable to intrusive signals from the rest of awareness.

Hypnotic induction

Hypnotic induction refers to employing a series of preliminary instructions and suggestions to draw someone into hypnosis.

Key features of hypnosis:

Concentrated attention to a single object or idea

Isolation from peripheral awareness

Increased reception to suggestions

Dark vs white hypnosis

The difference between white and dark hypnosis rests in the intent of the hypnotist. Dark hypnosis is intended to exploit the hypnotic person for selfish gains by the hypnotist.

White hypnosis is intended to improve the condition of the hypnotic by helping the hypnotic snap out from a traumatic or harmful state of consciousness.

Hypnotherapy is the most common type of white hypnosis. White hypnosis is often referred to as therapeutic hypnosis.

Hypnotherapy

Hypnotherapy is a form of white hypnotic induction practiced by medical practitioners for therapeutic purposes. The main aim is to help a patient heal from psychological, emotional, emotional, and even physical trauma.

Hypnotherapy can be used in pain relief in such a manner that enables the patient to dissociate himself from the source of the pain thus lessening sensitivity to that pain.

Facts about hypnosis:

- It is voluntary

- It is willful

- Children are more susceptible to hypnotism than adults

- 15% of people are highly susceptible to hypnotism

- 10% of people can hardly be hypnotized

- Those people who are easily absorbed in fantasies are more susceptible to hypnotism

Negative effects of Dark hypnotic induction

There are many victims of dark hypnotic induction. The following are some of the common causes of dark hypnotic induction:

- Being hypnotized to such an extent that you willfully give your possession to the hypnotist

- Being hypnotized such that you willfully open your door to robbers

- Being hypnotized such that you voluntarily follow kidnappers to their den

Psychological manipulation

Psychological manipulation is the act of employing deceptive, abusive or underhanded tactics to change a person's perception or behavior.

THE FOUR DARK PERSONALITY CLASSIFICATIONS

After a thorough rundown of what Dark Psychology is and how it affects society as a whole, let's delve into the specific classifications with the dark psyche. There are hundreds of terms to describe dark psyche actions. We listed the nine major traits related to dark psyches in recent chapters. These traits are sometimes obvious, and other times very difficult to pinpoint, especially when you are faced with them head-on. It is important, that you understand these traits in order to understand why there are four major classifications in Dark Psychology.

These traits are often the initial tell-tale signs when psychologists begin to treat a patient. They are looking for specific qualities that an individual exhibits on a regular basis. Once these traits are listed and quantified, the diagnosis then can move forward. These types of diagnosis can be difficult since many of the classifications of dark personalities have interwoven characteristics. On top of that, not all of the traits are equally brandished by the patient. Therefore, a deeper look into the behaviors of that patient needs to be taken into account.

Despite the complexity of diagnosis by a licensed professional, on a personal level, you will be able to understand the specific characteristics that dark personalities often carry. This will help you to spot the dangerous red flags that we can often miss when interacting with a person.

Spitefulness

Spitefulness dates back to even before human beings existed. In fact, spite has been studied within organisms in order to further understand the relevance in the human species. In the land of ash and fire, when the Earth was transitioning into a greener and more livable space, organisms were forming deep in the watery depths of the oceans. Some of these organisms had a reactionary defense that released toxins that killed the other organisms. In doing so, however, those same toxins often killed the releaser. Ever heard the saying, "cut off your nose to spite your face?"

S.A. West, A.S. Griffin, and A. Gardner, the authors of

the study entitled, Social Semantics: Altruism, Cooperation, Mutualism, Strong Reciprocity, and Group Selection from the Institute of Evolutionary Biology defined Spite as, "a behavior in which is beneficial to the actor and costly to the recipient." But what this definition does not include is the fact that spite quite often backfires in the "actor's" face.

Self-Interest

Self-interest is pretty simple to explain in normal terms. It is simply putting yourself before all others despite the cost to the other party. In psychology, there are two subsets of self-interest, egoism and narcissism which will be explained below. Within the philosophical realm of self-interest, there are several concepts behind self-interest.

- Enlightened Self-Interest- This concept states that if you do for others, ultimately you will be serving your own self-interest as well.

- Ethical Egoism- This concept is the thought that people should do what is best for themselves.

- Rational Egoism- This belief centers around the idea that any rational action that you take should always be done in your own self-interest.

- Hedonism- Hedonism makes the assertion that the only type of good is pleasure. Hedonism also includes the pre-Socratic Cyrenaics and the philosophical system known as Epicureanism.

- Individualism- This is a philosophy that teaches people to have a very strong sense of self-worth.

Psychopathy

The term psychopath is a commonly used word in society and doesn't often fully encompass the reality of the mental disorder. Psychopaths are too often written off as patients that do not hold the capability to be treated. However, this is not true in a majority of the cases. Like so many other mental illnesses through the years, they are often tossed into a mental institution and forgotten about. The psychological world is beginning to change that trend. This will be discussed further below.

Psychological Entitlement

Psychological Entitlement is a term that has become more and more well known in today's society. It is the belief that some people deserve more than others. Through history, we have seen entitlement between financial classes, races, sexes, and even religious institutions. A sense of entitlement can come from your background, your surroundings, the teachings you had growing up, and just an innate inner belief that you should have more because you are better than others. Psychological entitlement can also be seen within the workplace. When someone is more educated, has had a longer time on the job, or even has a higher title than others, they can develop a sense of self-worth that makes them believe they are more important than others and therefore, more deserving of things like better pay and easier tasks. Psychological Entitlement is a trait that is usually burrowed deep into someone's psyche. It can be hard to break but it is possible through regular treatment programs. However, many people overlook entitlement on a deep seeded psychological level because they assume it is simply a product of the environment, not a mental illness that needs to be treated.

Narcissism

Narcissism is a trait that, though healthy in small children, can become dangerous if it is developed after puberty. Narcissists are incredibly selfish and always have some sort of sense of entitlement. Narcissists always lack empathy, and crave attention and admiration from everyone around them. They are usually very good at getting their way, and often talk circles around arguments in order to confuse the other person and remove blame from themselves. Narcissists can be found in all walks of life, from high political offices to the neighbor down the street. Narcissistic behavior is not only dangerous to the people it is aimed at but can be dangerous to the aggressor as well. Narcissism will be discussed in greater depth later in this chapter.

Moral Disengagement

Moral Disengagement is a term related to social psychology. It is the act of convincing your own mind that ethical and moral standards don't apply to you. A person suffering from moral disengagement is able to disconnect the part of the brain that tells them what they are doing is wrong. They often are part of inhumane activities to which they justify through verbally recited morals, comparison to others, removing responsibility from themselves, shrugging of serious injuries to others as if they weren't as bad as they seemed, and one of the worst, they immediately begin to dehumanize the person in which they have acted against.

One not so talked about form of moral disengagement is used in military tactic on a daily basis. The military morally justifies the killing of "enemies" for the greater good of society. They go so far as to convince the soldiers that their actions made them heroes. And this does not just happen to the members of the military, but to society as well when we shake the hand of a soldier and justify the actions they took because we've been told that there is some sort of moral caveat when it comes to enemy lives.

Machiavellianism

Machiavellianism is a personality type that encompasses manipulation. Those that fall under this type are often master manipulators without ever even knowing it. Their temperament exposes them to be deceptive, conniving, and for all intents and purposes, amoral. Machiavellianism will be discussed more in length below.

Egoism

Psychological egoism within a personality creates a belief that every motive you have is for the betterment of yourself. Egoists are often considered nonmoral and do not all operate in the same fashion. There is no specific, verifiable course or personality that an egoist takes but the base of their person cares for themselves first over all others.

Now that we understand some of the major traits within Dark Psychology, we will be able to better pinpoint why the following four are more often diagnosed on a clinical level. They can arguably also be some of the worst Dark Personality traits you could have.

Psychopaths

Psychopaths are those that suffer, ultimately, from psychopathy. They have a tendency to have multiple diagnoses and can exhibit strange, and often violent behavior. When you hear or read the word psychopath, almost everyone has some sort of image pop into their mind. Whether it is Michael Myers inhumanly walking at a glacial pace always catching up to the screaming girl, or the face of Norman Bates as he flaunts his mother's most beautiful dress while slaughtering people, the word brings a connotation of fear and horror.

TECHNIQUES OF DARK PSYCHOLOGY

Persuasion

The first thing that we need to take a look at here is what a dark persuader is all about. If you look through the dictionary, it is going to talk about how persuasion is to prevail on someone to do or to believe something using a number of methods, often with reasoning and advising. This may seem pretty much the same things as regular persuasion, but the difference is that intention that comes with the persuasion. Basically, persuasion is when you are going to use reason and other techniques in order to get someone to do what you want, whether that is for the good of the other person or not. Let's take a closer look at what persuasion is all about, and how we are able to use this for our own needs.

There are six main elements that come with persuasion and understanding how these do work is how the manipulator is able to use persuasion for their needs. These are also kind of like the techniques that you are able to use for persuasion, and you are able to bring these out in order to help you see some success with what you can do with the other person. Some of the different techniques that can be used when it comes to persuasion and making it work for you include:

Reciprocity

The first tactic to use will be an idea that is known as reciprocity. This is going to be a principle that works on the idea that when someone does a favor for us, or provides us with something of value, no matter how big or small that item or action may be, we are going to try and repay them, and pay off our "debt" to them in some manner. Oftentimes, the item or favor that the persuader offer is going to be smaller than the thing they want from us. But because they offered us something, often without us asking for it, and they helped us out with a task of some sort, and then asked for their turn right after, we are the target are more likely to agree to help, even if we really don't want to.

When a dark persuader brings out the ideas that come with reciprocation, the point is that they want to create some sort of obligation in the target to agree, which is going to be a very powerful and effective tool to use with persuasion. The reciprocity rule is going to be this effective because it can be really overbearing to us, and we don't want to seem ungrateful for the help or like we are shrugging off our duties. And so we end up agreeing to help out, without a ton of push from the persuader in the first place.

If you are using this technique, you will find that the item or the favor that you offer to the other person is going to be pretty small. You may run to the office in order to make some copies for them or grab them a coffee when you are already going up. But once you are done with this small thing, and you have helped them out, it is the perfect time for you to ask them to help you with something that you want. Keep in mind that the sooner you ask for your favor after you are done helping, the more likely it is that you will be able to get the target to agree to do what you want, even if your request is much larger than the thing you helped them out with.

Commitment and Consistency

Once you have worked with the idea of reciprocity for a bit, it is time to move on to commitment and consistency. Consistency is an important part of society and relationships, and it can be important when it comes to persuasion because:

- It is something that society is going to value quite a bit.

- It is going to provide us with a beneficial approach to our daily life.

- It is able to provide us with a valuable shortcut through some of the complicated parts of our modern way of life.

Consistency works because it is going to allow us to become more effective at making our decisions and processing the information that we receive. The concept of consistency is going to state that when someone commits to doing something, whether they commit through writing or by speaking. They are more likely to honor the commitment that they made.

This is going to be especially true when something is written down because this ensures that the evidence is more concrete and this gives the person the hard proof that they need to really fix the issues that they need. Someone who commits to a stance tends to behave according to the commitment that they agree to.

You will find that this commitment is going to be a

really effective technique to use with persuasion because once you are able to get the other person to commit, then they are more likely to engage in the form of self-persuasion providing themselves and others with the justifications and the reasons to support their commitment in order to avoid some of the other issues that can come up with not following the commitment. If you are able to get the other person to make this commitment in front of a group or at least one other person, then you will find that you will be able to persuade them to do something even more readily.

Social Proof

The third technique that we are going to take a look at is known as social proof. As humans, we find that the people around us are really going to influence us in many aspects. Even if we want to be unique and do things on our own terms, there is always going to be someone who will influence you in some way. We want those in our lives to like us, we want to be seen as acceptable in our group, and we want to do and have what other people do. It may surprise us to find out how much our beliefs and our actions are based on what others are doing in our own social groups.

This idea is going to be like following the power of the crowd, and a persuader is going to find that it can be a nice tactic to use. We all want to know what those near us and around us are doing. This is often going to be the most effective when the other person is uncertain about the area around them, such as when they are in a new location they have never been. When the situation is uncertain, or when the situation presents someone with more than one choice to make, it is likely that we are going to conform to what others are doing around us to help us make our decisions.

What this means is that if you are interested in influencing those around you, then you need to be able to show the target that others around them, the other people they want to be like and admire, are doing the same course that you are suggesting. Convince them that everyone is doing it, that this is what they need to do to be seen as cool and to fit in with society, and more, and you will be able to convince the target to do what you would like.

Likeness

We can also work a bit with the persuasion element of likeness. This is a principle that is pretty concise and simple to work with, but it still brings in a lot of power to your tactics and techniques with the target. People are often going to say yes more often when they are talking to someone they like. But if they don't find the other person likable that they just met, or they don't like someone they have known for a while, it is much easier to tell that person no when they ask for some help.

When it comes to the likeability of someone, there are a few factors that we can consider with this one to determine if a target is going to instantly like you or not. We will just limit our focus here to the two major factors that you can concentrate on. The first factor to consider is whether or not the target is going to find you physically attractive. This sounds shallow and may seem a bit silly, but it is definitely something that is going to be true with your target, and because of this, you can use this idea to your advantage any time you want to use persuasion on your target.

When the target finds that you are physically

attractive, they will automatically agree with you, and you will find that you are more persuasive with them. Those who have better looks physically, no matter how shallow it sounds, are going to be able to get what they want from others, without even really needing to try. Physical attractiveness is able to send a message to your target and can even make the target think you have other good traits including talent, intelligence, and kindness, even if you haven't taken the time to show any of these characteristics, and even if you don't even have them.

The second factor that we need to consider with likeness is the idea of similarity. It is true that your target is so much easier to persuade to do what you want when they feel that you and they are similar to one another in some manner. If you pay attention to their body language and actually listen to what they are trying to tell you when they speak, you will find that it is so much easier to match up your personality and cues to theirs. And this helps make it so that your target sees the two of you as similar, and decides to listen to you.

Authority

Authority is a very effective method that you are able to use in order to get the other person to listen to you and to do what you would like. We all are going to have some kind of tendency to believe an expert if they say something. We think that if they tell us some facts or some information then it needs to be true and we should believe what they are saying. People like to find a quick way to make decisions, and they like listening to those who are trustworthy and knowledgeable about the topic at hand. If you are able to bring out both of those and show it off to the target, then you will be able to get others to believe and listen to you.

You need to make sure that you are able to convince the other person that you are the authority figure. If you are able to do this, they are going to come to you for advice, and they will believe that the advice that you give them is going to be in their best interest and that they need to listen to you. Whether or not it is actually going to be in their best interests is not going to matter to the persuader, but it does help them to get the results that they want.

Scarcity

This is going to be considered one of the best and most effective methods of persuasion that you are able to use against one of your targets when you want to get your goals. When something appears to have a limited amount of availability, and won't be around for long, it seems like people are going to give it more value than it is worth. The reason for this higher value is because people want to get more of what they are not able to have. When you can manipulate the system so that you can make scarcity a real issue, then the target is going to want to rush right towards that item or the path that you are suggesting and get it for themselves.

What this is going to mean for you as the persuader is that, within the right context, scarcity is going to help you reach your goals. In order to get people to believe that an item or a chosen path is scarce, they need to get their hands on it right now, for example, the marketer is going to explain what the product does and why it is so much better at it than anything else on the market. Another approach is telling the customer what they are likely to lose out on if they choose not to go with that item, rather than talking just about the benefits. So, you may avoid saying something like, "You will save $5 by using it," and instead you would go with something like, "You will lose $5." The second option is going to bring up the idea of scarcity a bit more and can make the target run to get that item.

Now, you will find that the persuasion tactic of scarcity is going to be effective and powerful, and there are a number of reasons for this one. Some of the biggest reasons that the scarcity tactic works so well include:

When it is hard to get something that people are going to see it as more valuable. This makes it seem like that item is going to be higher in quality even though that doesn't have to be true.

When things start to have a limited amount of availability, this means that we are going to lose the chance in the future to get them, and we don't want to miss out.

The idea that we get with this one is that we want to get anything that we think it out of our reach, or will be gone soon because it is rare. We want to stand out, or we don't want to miss out on something. If we notice that there is a path we can come back to later, or that there is a deal that is always around, then we won't put as much value on it. But when something seems like it is rare and going to be gone soon, then we give it more value, and we want it more. This is how the idea of scarcity is going to work with your target.

This is going to be helpful when we are looking at persuasion. If we are able to convince the other person that what we are offering or what we have to say and want them to do, is rare or only available for a short amount of time, then they are more likely to agree to it. This doesn't work all of the time, but it has a higher level of success and will ensure that you are more likely to get what you want out of that other person.

These six techniques of persuasion are going to be some of the best that you can use to get the results that we want from our target. These persuasion techniques take some time to learn, and we have to be able to use them in the proper manner to ensure that we convince the target to do what we want, rather than choosing their own course of action. But you will find that, while these techniques are going to seem pretty simple, and the ideas that come with them are not that hard to learn, they are going to be effective and can be modified and pulled out no matter who your target is, or what situation you are dealing with, which makes them some of the best dark psychology techniques to use to get what you want from others.

Manipulation

Manipulation is the act of utilizing backhanded strategies to control conduct, feelings, and connections.

What Is Manipulation?

The vast majority participates in occasional control. For instance, telling a colleague you feel "fine" when you are really discouraged is, in fact, a type of control since it controls your associate's view of and responses to you.

Control can likewise have progressively guileful outcomes, notwithstanding, and it is frequently connected with psychological mistreatment, especially in private connections. The vast majority see control contrarily, particularly when it hurts the physical, enthusiastic, or psychological wellness of the individual being controlled.

While individuals who control others regularly do as

such in light of the fact that they want to control their condition and environment, an urge that frequently originates from profound situated dread or uneasiness, it is anything but solid conduct. Participating in control may keep the controller from associating with their credible self, and being controlled can make an individual encounter a wide scope of sick impacts.

Psychological Well-Being Effects of Manipulation

In the event that unaddressed, control can prompt poor emotional wellness results for the individuals who are controlled. Incessant control in cozy connections may likewise be a sign psychological mistreatment is occurring, which at times, can have a comparable impact to injury—especially when the casualty of control is made to feel regretful or embarrassed.

Casualties of incessant control may:

- Feel discouraged

- Develop nervousness

- Develop undesirable adapting designs

- Constantly attempt to satisfy the manipulative individual

- Lie about their emotions

- Put someone else's needs before their own

- Find it hard to confide in others

Now and again, control can be inescapable to such an extent that it makes an injured individual inquiry their view of the real world. The exemplary motion picture Gaslight outlined one such story, in which a lady's significant other quietly controlled her until she never again confided in her very own discernment. For instance, the spouse clandestinely turned down the gaslights and persuaded his better half the diminishing light was all in her mind.

Control and Mental Health

While the vast majority take part in control now and again, an unending example of control can demonstrate a fundamental psychological wellness concern.

Control is especially basic with character issue analyses, for example, marginal character (BPD) and narcissistic character (NPD). For some with BPD, control might be methods for gathering their passionate needs or acquiring approval, and it frequently happens when the individual with BPD feels shaky or surrendered. The same number of individuals with BPD have seen or experienced maltreatment, control may have created as a method for dealing with stress to get necessities met by implication.

People with narcissistic character (NPD) may have various explanations behind taking part in manipulative conduct. As those with NPD may experience issues framing cozy connections, they may depend on control so as to "keep" their accomplice in the relationship. Qualities of narcissistic control may incorporate disgracing, accusing, playing the "person in question," control issues, and gaslighting.

Munchausen disorder as a substitute, during which a parental figure makes someone else sick to pick up consideration or fondness, is another condition that is described by manipulative practices.

Control in Relationships

Long haul control can have genuine impacts in cozy connections, including those between companions, relatives, and sentimental accomplices. Control can decay the strength of a relationship and lead to the poor psychological well-being of those in the relationship or even the disintegration of the relationship.

In a marriage or association, control can make one accomplice feel harassed, segregated, or useless. Indeed, even in solid connections, one accomplice may coincidentally control the other so as to evade showdown or even trying to shield their accomplice from inclination loaded. Numerous individuals may even realize they are being controlled in their relationship and neglect or make light of it. Control in personal connections can take numerous structures, including embellishment, blame, blessing giving or specifically indicating warmth, mystery keeping, and latent hostility.

Guardians who control their kids may set their kids up for blame, wretchedness, uneasiness, eating issues, and other emotional wellness conditions. One investigation likewise uncovered that guardians who normally use control strategies on their kids may improve the probability their youngsters will likewise utilize manipulative conduct. Indications of control in the parent-youngster relationship may incorporate making the tyke feel regretful, absence of responsibility from a parent, minimizing a tyke's accomplishments, and a should be associated with numerous parts of the kid's life.

Individuals may likewise feel controlled in the event that they are a piece of a kinship that has turned out to be harmful. In manipulative fellowships, one individual might utilize the other to address their very own issues to the detriment of their friend's. A manipulative companion may utilize blame or intimidation to concentrate favors, for example, crediting cash, or they may possibly contact that companion when they need their very own passionate needs met and may discover pardons when their companion has needs in the relationship.

Instances of Manipulative Behavior

Here and there, individuals may control others unknowingly, without being completely mindful of what they are doing, while others may effectively chip away at reinforcing their control strategies. A few indications of control include:

- Passive-forceful conduct

- Implicit dangers

- Dishonesty

- Withholding data

- Isolating an individual from friends and family

- Gaslighting

- Verbal misuse

- Use of sex to accomplish objectives

As the thought processes behind control can change from oblivious to pernicious, it is imperative to distinguish the conditions of the control that is occurring. While severing things might be basic in circumstances of maltreatment, an advisor may help other people figure out how to manage or face manipulative conduct from others.

Instructions to Deal with Manipulative People

At the point when control ends up lethal, managing the conduct from others can be debilitating. Control in the working environment has been appeared to diminish execution and manipulative conduct from friends and family can cause reality to appear to be faulty. On the off chance that you believe you are being controlled in any sort of a relationship, it might be useful to:

- Disengage. In the event that somebody is attempting to get a specific enthusiastic reaction from you, decide not to offer it to them. For instance, if a manipulative companion is known to compliment you before requesting overextending support, don't play along—rather, answer courteously and move the discussion along.

- Be certain. Some of the time, control may incorporate one individual's endeavors to make someone else question their capacities, instinct, or even reality. In the event that this occurs, it might adhere to your story; in any case, if this happens regularly in a cozy relationship, it could be an ideal opportunity to leave.

- Address the circumstance. Get out the manipulative conduct as it is going on. Maintaining the attention on how the other individual's activities are influencing you as opposed to beginning with an accusatory proclamation may likewise enable you to arrive at a goal while underlining that their manipulative strategies will not take a shot at you.

- Stay on-point. When you call attention to conduct that makes you feel controlled, the other individual may attempt to limit the circumstance or jumble the circumstance by raising different issues as a diversion. Keep in mind your primary concern and adhere to that.

Types of Manipulation

There are several types of manipulation because it can often depend on where the manipulator is or who they are manipulating. For example, there are some manipulators who focus on workplace tactics while others will manipulate their significant other. Of course, there are manipulators who will use their tactics no matter where they are or who they are with.

Covert Emotional Manipulation

Covert emotional manipulation is a part of any form of manipulation. However, it is stronger in people who are known as "master manipulators" or people who will manipulate anyone in order to get anything they want. It is not as strong in manipulation tactics people use when they tell someone they are fine, even though something is wrong.

At the base of manipulation is working to change the way people feel and think, which is covert emotional manipulation. They focus on your conscious awareness in order to control you. Because of this, people don't often realize that they are being manipulated.

First, the manipulator will get you to trust them. Then, they will start to control the way you feel, think, and perceive situations. This will happen slowly as they don't want you to catch on to the manipulation. Once they feel that your emotions and thoughts are in their hands, they will start to tear apart your confidence. A master manipulator knows they have to lower your self-esteem in order to control you the way they want to. They will also work to take away your identity, which allows you to fully become theirs.

While they are trying to break you down emotionally and mentally, they will also try to keep you away from your family and friends. One of the biggest reasons for this is people who knew you before they came into your life are a threat to them. Your family and friends will notice a change in you, and they won't like it. They will try to find out why you are changing and, typically very quickly, they point their fingers at the manipulator. When this happens, your friends and family will do what they can to try to see what this person is doing to you and how you are being treated. This is one of the most common signs of manipulation in relationships.

Of course, you will start to notice a change within yourself. Unfortunately, it is usually after the manipulator has had control over you. You start to notice yourself change when you begin to feel different. You might notice you have anxiety, you are depressed, having trouble sleeping, you struggle trusting people you once trusted, and you have become increasingly isolated ("About Covert Emotional Manipulation", n.d.).

For most people, it is hard to spot the signs of manipulators. This is especially true for people who suffer from manipulation from their significant other. In general, it is hard to spot certain signs of manipulation. Furthermore, it is often harder to spot these behaviors from people who you love and believe love you back. In relationships, people often turn a "blind eye" to their significant other's manipulative ways because they see them as faults. We work to understand the faults of each other in relationships.

While you will want to notice the personality traits of a manipulator discussed previously, there are a lot of other signs when it comes to manipulation in relationships. This is because manipulators often let down their guard a bit when they are at home. They are in their comfort zone and believe they can do anything, and you won't protect yourself or try to change it because you are too weak.

1. They will start a fight with you over something minor.

Manipulators need to win, and this is frequently displayed in their relationships, especially their romantic ones. Therefore, you may notice that if you are having a minor disagreement with your significant other, they will turn it into a fight so that you allow them to win. They want you to give up and do whatever they want to do.

2. They are great secret keepers.

While they don't like it when you keep any secret from them, they can keep anything they want from you. Furthermore, they don't have to tell you anything they are doing or where they are going. This simply doesn't matter to you. In other words, what they do is their business and you need to mind your own.

However, if you treat them the same way, they will start a fight, tell you that you don't love them, or become angry. This is because if they don't know everything about you, they are losing their control. They are also able to keep control away from you by not letting you know their secrets.

3. Their actions and words don't match.

Manipulators realize that in order to keep you in their control, they need to sometimes give you what you want. While this can come in the form of gifts, they will usually focus on telling you what you want to hear. However, they will not follow through with their words. For example, if you are feeling lonely and don't want your significant other to go out with their friends again, you will ask them to stay with you. You will ask for time alone or to go with them. They will give you an excuse for why tonight won't work, but then make a promise to spend more time with you or both of you will do something another night. Unfortunately, they will rarely follow through with their promise.

4. They will act like the victim.

There is always a time that you are going to argue with your significant other or try to stand up for yourself. This not only happens in the beginning but throughout the relationship. When it does, the manipulator is going to play the role of the victim. They will twist your words to make it seem like you are the one who is doing something wrong. While you might not agree with this perception at first, they will continue to use their emotions to persuade you to believe them.

Manipulation in the Workplace

Many people deal with workplace manipulation at some point in their career. Sometimes it is because one of their co-workers is a manipulator while other times it is everyday forms of manipulation. For example, a co-worker manipulates you into helping them with their task or gets you to do their task. They only do this because they don't like this specific responsibility.

Sometimes you will start to notice your supervisor is a manipulator. Unfortunately, this is highly common in the workplace as many supervisors have used manipulation to get their position, especially if they worked themselves up the ladder. However, you should never assume your supervisor is manipulative. If they are, they will typically demonstrate signs of being a manipulator, such as bullying, blaming others, guilting their staff, giving staff the silent treatment, and distorting facts.

One way you know if you work with a manipulator is by the way you are treated. Manipulators need to make sure you know your place, meaning you are beneath them. Therefore, they will often make sarcastic comments that make you feel inferior. For example, you come to work one day in professional attire that is more casual than your company usually wears. Instead of a white shirt and a suit, you are wearing a white shirt with slacks. When your co-worker notices your attire, they start to belittle your clothes, making fun of your lower-paying income and that you can't afford nicer clothes.

When Can Manipulation Be Positive?

Manipulation is a valuable tool, just like a hammer and nails can be. You can either use the hammer, or the manipulation, to destroy something or you can use these tools to create something new and useful. The act of having all this control over a situation or other people can be a compelling position. That power can be used for bad, but it can also be used for good.

For example, let's say that you see a piece of paper laying around that has the username and password for the boss's computer. You could choose to throw the paper away and not use it, or you can log in to the computer and look up the information that is on there. If you find that someone left their wallet behind in the bathroom, you could take the cash and throw the wallet away without anyone knowing, or you can turn it into the front desk.

Those examples are sometimes a little more clear cut. We know what the right thing is and what the wrong thing is. And most of us are going to pick the right one and stick with what is good. But a manipulator would do the option that benefited them the most. They would use manipulation to find the weaknesses of someone else and then exploit these things. But you could also use these weaknesses as a way to improve the life of the victim and encourage these individuals any time that they feel weak.

No matter who you are, most people are going to choose to use manipulation to their advantage, and in the wrong hands, this can be a dangerous behavior it is important to note that not everyone who exhibits some of the qualities of a manipulative person is using it negatively. Some people may see that this is a tactic for their survival. Others may use it because they think that they know what is best for the other person, rather than just trying to trick them.

An excellent example of positive manipulation, or at least manipulation that isn't meant to be evil or bad, is that of children. All children use some level of manipulation, but this doesn't mean the children are evil. This is merely because they are learning how they should interact with other people. They will learn how to make changes based on the responses that they get from others in their little world.

Positive social influence

Now, let's take a look at some of the ways that manipulation can be turned into a positive thing. First, we will look at social influence. This is how our society, as well as the people that are around us, have developed ideas that will influence the individuals in those institutions. Things like ethics, morality, religion, and social norms are going to be in this group, and they can affect how we interact and shape our personal views.

There are going to be three varieties of social influence. The first one is going to be compliance, which means that you would keep your opinions to yourself, even if they happen to be different than what others have. The second one is going to be identification. This is going to be the influence of someone that is respected and admired. And then there is the third one that is known as internalization. This is when a belief, behavior, or an idea is accepted, and everyone in that society or group agrees to it privately and publicly.

Social influence can be a good thing, but there are times when it can be harmful to the victim and others as well. When it is good, it could be a doctor who is using some persuasion to help ensure their patient does the right treatment to get healthy. They will believe that there is a specific medication that is best to treat a certain disease. Because of this, they will work on manipulation to convince their patient to take that medication; without any other motives or personal gain, outside of the patient getting better.

Another example of good social influence is when there are some campaigns done to help educate users on certain things that need to be changed in society. Think about those commercials that try to get people to stop smoking. They can be manipulative sometimes, and they often exaggerate the truth a bit to get the person to stop. There is usually some fear tactics as well. The manipulation isn't there to help the advertiser benefit. It is there to try and get the individual to stop smoking and to improve their health.

Not all manipulators you encounter are going to be evil.

Just because someone you know is labeled as a manipulator, this doesn't mean that they are already an evil person and you should never have anything to do with them. Everyone has a different motive for trying to manipulate others around them. There are always better ways that you can confront issues rather than using the tactics of manipulation, but for some people, these tactics are the only way they know how to handle the problems.

Many manipulators are not aware of the proper means to express their emotions. So instead of trying to work with the situation at hand in a more constructive manner, they are going to use the tactics of manipulation to get what they want.

Let's take a look at this differently. There is a girl who sees that her sister is struggling through many aspects of her life. Maybe the sister is having trouble with her classes in college, is addicted to drugs or alcohol, and is having trouble paying her bills. The girl could decide to use some of the tactics to work on getting her sister to change these behaviors.

Does this make the first girl evil? She may be using the manipulation techniques that we talked about before, but the result is that she wants what is best for her sister. And maybe in the process, she believes that tricking her sister into doing something would end up with both of them getting better results in the process.

Manipulation is usually a form of avoiding a bigger truth. Maybe a wife would use some humor to joke about the way that your husband's hair looks, but she needs to be more honest and come out and tell him he needs a haircut. It is possible that the husband is not going to agree with this, but at least if the wife is honest, the husband isn't going to be made to feel like less by the cruel humor.

There are many times when manipulation can be used as a way to improve a person or improve society. It has gained a very negative connotation over the years because of how most manipulators use it. But overall, it is a great option that can be used to make things better, and even benefit other people that you know. You need to learn how to use it properly to get these results.

Mind Control

Mind control is at its heart the notion that certain psychological methods can alter or regulate the human mind. This practice is said to decrease the capacity of its subject to believe critically or independently, to allow the entry into the mind of the subject of fresh, unwanted thoughts and ideas, and to alter its attitudes, values, and beliefs.

To manipulate, reforming thought, brainwashing, coercive persuasion and control and abuses in group dynamics, are also considered versions of mind control. The fact that so many names exist shows a lack of consensus that makes confusion and distortion possible.

Forensic psychologist Dick Anthony, 2003

In 2016, Van Leer Jerusalem Institute member Adam Klin-Oron,who is also an Israeli religion anthropologist said of the "anti-proposed" And ultimately, judges dismissed expert witnesses, including in Israel, who claimed there was "brainwashing."Cults usually execute all or some of these techniques to recruit and gain followers.

Once a follower is gained, these tools are also use to control them. Cults may use these following techniques:

- Chanting and singing

- Isolation

- Dependency and fear

- Activity and pedagogy

- Sleep deprivation and fatigue

- Self-criticism and finger pointing

- Love bombing

- Mystical manipulation

- Thought termination

The first technique is chanting and singing. Singing mantras is an significant component in many religions, especially Buddhism and Hinduism, as well as other types of mass singing in every organization. As band employees, the phrases are sung or mantras in unison, with all of their voices becoming one, a robust sense of belonging and company distinctiveness builds. When the technique is used, a state of lowered heart rate and relaxation occurs. This occurrence may help cast the worshipping group practice in a constructive light. But the ongoing succession of brief phrasings in a cult is planned to become head-numbing, eradicate rational thought, and establish a state of mood.

Psychologists Linda Dubrow-Marshall and Steve Eichel

Group control using singing and chanting is manipulated by cult leaders to break the individuality, and critical thinking abilities of a person instead of meditative purposes.

Isolation is the second technique. Physical isolation give cults the farther advantage of mind control by moving people away from external influences, such as relatives and loved ones. Public events, such as group meetings and social events with other members can be beneficial and effective for the cult's message to be conveyed. Forced solitary confinement, both as punishment and a conditioning tool is used to strengthen control though isolation. A slower way of building a relationship and persuading to isolate the individual away from outside forces is by establishing a one on one relationship. As long as there are not any dissuading messages are seen or heard, emotional isolation will soon follow physical isolation.

Without the outside influences of friends and families, a cult can use this as proof that the individual is unwanted.

Hearst was abducted in 1974. during her captivity, she was subjected to abuse, both physical and psychological. Through this conditioning using dependency and fear, she quickly ended up becoming an associate of her captors, who may of taken advantage of her age and reputation (she came from a rather influential family), even participating in an armed back robbery. Her continual refusal of her being brainwashed when asked during her arrest hindered her defense. She was sentenced to prison for seven years, but her sentence was reduced.

Activity and pedagogy are also techniques. Several cults use this, in which they assign or encourage members to perform endless series of activities, such as physical labor or exercise to make the individual tired and exhausted both mentally and physically in order to lower their mental defenses and resolve, which will make them more susceptible. The activities are performed in a group setting, where the individual is never left alone or given any private time. Usually the activity is performed over and over again in repetition. The activity may also be of an academic nature, such as attending a long lecture or study. The leader or a trusted follower may be the "instructor".

What makes physical pedagogy different from regular sports is that the cult will take advantage of the group mentality to showcase certain ideological beliefs, which might be met with skepticism if the prospect were awake and alert.

As an example, Russia hosted mass sporting events for their citizens where they had to participate in physical activity.

In the 1970s, the followers of Jim Jones would work constantly on various duties for the church, It was usually for several days straight. If followers quit or stopped, they would be shamed or threatened.

The next technique is sleep deprivation. Sleep deprivation explains itself. Individuals are not allowed to sleep or rest, which in turn, harms the ability to make good decisions and be more susceptible. Activities such as weekend long events or functions, such as lectures which go on through the night which may include loud music or flashing lights to keep followers awake. Keepings followers on a strict diet containing low protein and other nutrients can also lead members to have low blood sugar, continuing their fatigue. Limiting sleep or rest can contribute to this too.

A former follower of the Aum Shinrikyo described that while campaigning to get their leader elected to parliament, they consumed one meal each day and slept only one to two hours every night.

Self-criticism and shaming is a technique where the group of followers denounce each other, talk about their own faults, leading to feelings of inadequacy and self-doubts, which in turn can lead to a dependency to the cult or group in an effort to "be fixed".

An example of this would be the experience of POWs during the Korean War. The Chinese forced them to participate in sessions where they would talk about their own faults and insecurity about capitalism and the US. These ongoing "discussions" began to work a little and the POWs began to question their own patriotism and their own self-worth. In the end, these sessions were unsuccessful, since only 23 POWs refused repatriotism and the Chinese abandoned their brainwashing program.

Love bombing is an effective technique in which the cult will make them appear welcoming and inviting by using the principle influence of recipocracy by showering potential recruits with affection and attention, since we are more inclined to feel like we must reciprocate the same affection and love. Love bombing is meant to create a sense of debt and obligation. When the generosity is not returned, the individual is supposed to feel guilty and it may reinforce devotion.

Not all attempts at love bombing are negative. Members of the Unification church use this technique as an expression of friendship, interest, concern or interest in a welcoming way. Other churches and organizations such as twelve step programs in which combat addictions practice love bombing as a way to welcome already vulnerable individuals in a genuine and real way as to build a welcoming atmosphere.

Mystical manipulation is a technique where the cult leader controls the information and circumstances in the group as to where it can be conveyed that the leader themselves can get their followers to believe that that they have supernatural or magical powers or divine favor by giving the false impression they give. The leaders claim that their word is indisputable and to question their words is to question the divine.

The final technique is thought terminating clichés. These are the uses and phrases, usually with rhetoric, that when used intensely, can help replace individual thoughts. The words and phrases, noted by Psychologist Robert Jay Lifton, were "all-encompassing jargon". The Soviet Union and China used this technique frequently.

Lifton considered their jargon to be:

"abstract, highly categorical, relentlessly judging"

and was, "the language of non-thought".

An interesting example of this technique was during the trial of Nazi official Adolf Eichman. When questioned, Eichman would constantly reply in stock phrases and clichés which pertained to National Socialism. The Soviet Union and China used this technique frequently. Eichman was so entrenched in the Nazi ideals, that it may have been virtually impossible for him to really understand the magnitude of his crimes, which is what mind control is all about: the complete and utter control of another living being.

Mind control, when used in the ways discussed are still used today. Sex traffickers use some of these techniques to gain a level of trust through feigning affection and generosity before beginning to monitor and control their actions and movements. They can prey on their prospective victims through promises of a great paying jobs, then instill dependency and fear using threats of deportation, involvement of law enforcement and deportation. Some victims may achieve a form of traumatic bonding or "Stockholm syndrome" with their captor or captors through prolonged imprisonment, which could lead to the victim's inability to seek assistance.

Mind control techniques, when used in the ways

discussed, can be abused to take advance of the vulnerability of the individual to make them more susceptible to the group's/leader/ other individual's needs or gains. Some of us may have wanted or may have been tempted to use these techniques in our daily lives (to make a boyfriend/spouse/ children more compliant, make it so our boss would give us a raise), what mind control takes away is the free will and independence of the person. That individuality at its core builds the character of that person.

BRAINWASHING TO STOP BEING MANIPULATED

Brainwashing tends to be a little more "personal" and subtle. Brainwashing often requires the victim to be isolated, and more dependent on the individual or group of individuals who are brainwashing them. This is a favorite tactic of cults, religious groups, and yes, even your favorite sports teams.

Let's focus on national, televised sports, the most seemingly innocent form of cult worship. Billions of people all over the world tune into to watch football, baseball, swimming, car racing, cricket, volleyball, curling... the list goes on. Those same billions spend even more billions of dollars on tickets and travel to live games, merchandise, and the access to watch their favorite teams on their favorite channel in the comfort of their own home. What would happen if the Super Bowl didn't air in February? An honest, logical guess might be: "The world would end as we know it." Championship games of all kinds draw larger audiences than political rallies, religious observations and even the release of the latest iPhone.

But let's see what happens: Does it really affect a fan's life if the Patriots win or lose the Super Bowl again? Not really, yet millions of television screens turn to the game every February regardless of their team affiliation. What kind of power is this?

A dangerous one, that's it. Just how the politician or businessman has a wide reach in order to emotionally manipulate an audience, large groups of brainwashers can wipe your conscious down to the bare essentials. Then it replaces that person's "personhood" with an identity, set of ideals, beliefs, likes and dislikes that aren't their own.

How is the NFL or NHL capable of Advertising and affiliations? The NFL is one of the largest and most prominent sponsors and advertisers of the United States military. Commercials for different branches play during breaks, certain games or national anthems are dedicated to veterans, POWs, or current individuals serving. Players even don camouflage, military-inspired gear as part of this relationship.

Then there was the debate over the national anthem when Colin Kaepernick knelt in solidarity for all of his fellow people of color brutalized by police violence. The NFL immediately launched a vociferous media campaign, that was picked up by NFL fans everywhere. Soon, stickers, hats and t-shirts could be found everywhere saying "I stand for the anthem."

The NFL took this opportunity to use their fan base's interests, as well as the hold on they already had on loyal fans. As television ratings were dropping, the NFL created a problem that didn't exist, turned it into a media tornado, and unleashed their rhetoric on millions of viewers nationwide. It had a discernible effect by creating a reason for people to watch other than for the game itself.

The Fundamentals of Brainwashing

Many people tend to get hypnosis, CEM, NLP and brainwashing confused. But brainwashing isn't just a dark psychological technique, but one identified by psychologists all over the world as well. It's not only a tool of sports teams, in fact, but it's also been the go-to method of acquiring members for cults for decades, if not centuries.

Brainwashing from here on out means the process of

forcing an individual into accepting belief systems completely and utterly different than their own, often under duress.

The simplest example to illustrate brainwashing are cults, or small groups of individuals who practice either a form of religion or other belief that from the outside looks a bit sketchy, questionable, and perhaps even evil. Some examples of famous cults and their leaders include:

Jim Jones, leader of the People's Temple Cult. Jones was a zealous religious leader who convinced hundreds of his followers to participate in a mass murder/suicide by drinking poisoned Kool-Aid.

Children of God/Family International, founded by David "Moses" Berg. Founded in California in 1968, members were encouraged to have sex with children to achieve "divinity." This cult still exists today on multiple continents and over 70 countries. This cult, in particular, was perpetuated by founder David Berg's master of propaganda writing and publishing, which drew new members to his group and kept older members close by.

Branch Davidians – This was a splintered extremist

group of Seventh Day Adventists that had been in existence since the 1950s. It wasn't until leader David Koresh took over as leader that he began to claim that he was the Messiah and claimed all women and female children for his own. The group did believe that the end of the world was nigh, but many never got to see it. The cult was disbanded in1993 after a standoff with FBI agents that resulted in more than 80 deaths.

Raëlism. Followers of this cult, founded in 1974, believe that all life on Earth is scientifically created, thus, not organic, and challenging all prevalent scientific theories of evolution. The Raël creator is named "Elohim" and that leaders within the movement are former aliens that will teach the earth how to carry on Raël traditions, including peace and mindfulness

Now that we have a few examples of cults, let's dissect what makes up a cult. Usually, this small, strange group will have one or two leaders with strong personalities that lead their followers and often make decisions on their behalf.

Cults also usually seem very accepting at first, but that's because they're looking to increase their numbers. Don't mistake friendliness for desperation on their part.

Cults also make followers feel safe. The boisterous and charming leader is also a comforter – those who end up lost or confused by traditional religion are comforted and brought into the fold. Existential questions like "Why am I here?" and "What is my purpose in life?" are easily answered by the cult's lore (usually a cult will have a few strong oral storytellers, too).

Acceptance. Purpose. Belonging. The things people crave most of all are the things cults are most willing to dish out.

Cults and Brainwashing

Cults and brainwashing go together like peanut butter and jelly. The latter enables the former. In this book and in this context, brainwashing is a type of total "reboot" of thought and framing of the mind. Again, unless the victim is perceptive, this technique will likely go unnoticed.

Before we return to cults, it's important to establish that this is not the only way brainwashing is used. For example, a dress code at your job could be brainwashing if you work there long enough for the brainwashing to work its way in. After working there long enough, you might believe that a certain length of the skirt is more appropriate than another or a style of shoes more "business casual" than just "casual." This can be harmful in the long run because the victim has internalized the self-reproach the dress-code encourages.

UNDETECTED MIND CONTROL

The term mind control has many definitions and interpretations, but the crucial thing to note is that it doesn't involve any sort of magic or supernatural ability; it just requires a rudimentary understanding of human emotions and behavior. Mind control can involve brainwashing a person, reeducating them, reforming their thoughts, using coercive techniques to persuade them of certain things, or brain-sweeping. There are many forms of mind control, and we could fill an entire book discussing all those forms, but for our purposes, we will look at the concept in general terms. Mind control means a person is trying to get others to feel, think, or behave in a certain way, or to react and make decisions following a certain pattern. It could vary from a girl trying to get her boyfriend to develop certain habits, to a cult leader trying to convince his followers that he is God.

Mind control is based on one thing: information. We have the thoughts and beliefs that we do because we learned them. When we are subjected to new information on a deliberate and consistent basis, it's possible to alter our beliefs, thoughts, or even memories. The brain is hardwired to survive, and towards that end, it's very good at learning information that is crucial for our survival. When you receive certain information consistently, your brain will start to believe it even if you know it's not true. For example, even if you are the most rational person out there, if you go online and watch 100 videos about a certain conspiracy theory, you will start to believe it to some extent. That explains why people who seem smart can end up getting indoctrinated into cults or even terrorist groups.

Mind control also works more effectively when one is dependent on the person who is trying to control his/her mind. Even in relationships that are involuntary, the victim can start buying the perpetrator's world view if they have been dependent on the perpetrator for a long time. That explains phenomena such as Stockholm syndrome (where people who are kidnapped or held hostage start being affectionate towards their captors and empathizing with their causes). The worst thing you can do is assume that you are too smart for mind control to work on you. Under the right circumstances, anyone can be persuaded to abandon their world view and adopt someone else's. Mind games are covert tricks that are deliberately crafted in order to manipulate someone. Think of them as "handcrafted" psychological manipulation techniques. While other techniques are applied broadly, mind games are created to target very specific people. They work best when the victim trusts the perpetrator, and the perpetrator understands the victim's personality and behavior. Most of the psychological manipulation techniques we have discussed thus far can be used when crafting mind games. A person who understands you will tell you certain things or behave in certain ways around you because they are deliberately trying to get you to react in a certain way. It almost always involves feigning certain emotions.

People who play mind games use innocent sounding communication to elicit calculated reactions from you. Psychologists refer to such mind games as "conscious one-upmanship," and they have observed that they occur in all areas of life. Mind games occur in office politics, personal relationships, and even in international diplomacy. At work, someone could try to make you feel like you are not up to the task so that they can steal an opportunity from you. In a marriage, your partner could make certain seemingly innocent slights against you so that you feel like you have something to prove, and you take a certain course of action as a result. In dating, there are "pickup artists" who use different kinds of tricks to get you to lower your guard and let them in. Mind control is not the whole of the vague information you hear in gossip, accompanied by conspiracy theories. It is the product of secret experiments with systematic studies dating back to World War II, perhaps older. Of course, the 20th-century totalitarian regimes, who wanted to robotize their subjects, also played a major role in this. Therefore, the first thing to note is that developing technology facilitates the mind-control efforts of the oppressors every year. Like Telegram scourge that happens today... But mind control; it is something that can be done without technology with the support of psychology and orator. The most striking example of this in history; this is the work carried out by Goebbels, the Minister of Propaganda of the Nazis. Goebbels succeeded in engraving his name in gold letters in this lane, which was the disgrace of humanity.

Mind control; It is the name given to all the unethical activities of some power centers to manage people in line with their goals, to shape their ideas and control their lifestyles. While technological opportunities can be utilized in mind control, human psychology, propaganda knowledge, and social engineering are essential. Also, mind control; it is applied in a highly systematic, insidious way by people who have done as much research as required by a master or doctor. In other words, it is essential that people don't realize the engineering applied to them, so to be hypnotized. Therefore, it is challenging to recognize and resist.

Effects of Mind Control on human

The effects of using mind control on human beings are seen in different ways. Some of them are as follows;

- "Memory loss and behavior disorders

- Change in direction, intensity and content of sound heard

- Speech deterioration by checking eyelids

- Severe heart palpitations

- Forcing accidents on the shoulders and arms during laborious work

- Jogging of the elbows and preventing work while doing something

- Pain and unnecessary movement of the legs, right and left swing and excessive stiffness

- Itching and blushing in hard-to-reach areas

- Contractions of large muscles in the back

- Checking hand gestures

- Reading thoughts or transmitting thoughts from outside

- Seeing moving imaginary images

- Keeping eyelids constantly open

- Continuous tinnitus

- Jaw and teeth shivering for no reason

THE POWER OF PERSUASION

At this point, you have had some time to analyze the target and figure out what makes them tick. You know whether they are driven more by logic or by emotions, and you know a lot more about what will work as a technique of manipulation for them. Once you are done with that, it is time to move into planting some of the seeds of how you would like the target to behave. These are hopefully going to get the target to agree to your course of action, but they are planted in a manner that makes it so the target feels they got to make the decision, rather than them feeling like they are forced to make the decision by someone else.

When all of that is done, it is time to move on to the third part of influence the process of persuading people. This is going to be the part that will require you to bring in some physical actions, rather than just using your words. These physical actions are so important because they will really push things over the edge and will get your target to agree with you, or get them to comply, with the thing you are asking for.

The trick to this one is that you need to use persuasion in a way that is going to work on your target. This is where the other two parts come in. if you were successful with all of this, and you really worked towards making the target understood then you will find that the persuading part of all of this was pretty easy. You will be well equipped to deal with the target because you will know the perfect tactic of persuasion that you can use each and every time.

Persuasion is such an important part of this. And we are going to take some time to explore how to make this work and some of the different techniques that come with persuasion later on. But right now, remember that persuasion is going to be a big part of the manipulation, and it is the step that will help to seal the deal. If you are able to put all three of these parts together, you will be amazed at the results that you are able to get from the target, and how easy it is to get them to do what you want.

This guidebook is going to spend some time working on the different techniques that you are able to use when it comes to the art of persuasion. This can sometimes be something that we see as a good thing. And often persuasion doesn't have the same evil or bad connotation that manipulation may, even though it is possible that it is going to be used for evil purposes along the way as well.

There is a lot of persuasions that we kind find in the world around us, and it is often going to depend again on the intention that is behind it, and how much choice the other person has. If they are able to see it working and then walk away without feeling any guilt or anything else in the process, then this is seen as a good form of persuasion that still lets you have some kind of choice. But if the manipulator, or the person behind the persuasion, is able to get you to behave in a certain way because it is really hard to walk away and say no, then this is often seen as a bad thing.

Think of some times when you have seen persuasion at work, and it didn't seem like such a bad thing to work with at all. You may have seen countless advertisements out there telling us to purchase this one product, and not another one. We may have had a parent or another family member try to convince us to do something because they needed help or because they thought that it was in our best interests.

We are able to see these kinds of manipulation and

find that they are not so bad. We are able to walk away from the advertisements on TV because we have seen a lot of them in our lives, and they all say the same thing over and over again. We know that when a family member, for the most part, tells us about a plan and how they want us to try something, we recognize that it is usually for something that is good for us and we are willing to consider doing something.

But then there are times when the manipulation may not be the best thing for us at all. We find that this persuasion is going to be used against us and that the answer and the reaction to it are not going to be able to benefit us really at all in the process. This is the type of persuasion that we need to be really careful about, the kind that can sometimes sneak up on us without us even knowing. And then we are going to end up losing our control and giving it to the person who is trying to manipulate us.

Staying secret when you manipulate

While we just talked a bit about the three steps or stages to influence, we also need to take a look at what can be known as the final part of this process. It is not really a step like the others but it is important to consider when you do manipulation. When you are working with this process, it is important for you to remember that your intentions need to be kept hidden as much as possible in order to see the results.

Think of it this way. How would you feel if you found out someone was trying to manipulate you against your will? It's likely that you would not feel the best, and would want to stay as far away from them as possible. If someone else finds out that you were working to manipulate them, there are going to be two different things that could show up.

First, it is likely that your target is going to stop trusting you. They will wonder how many other things you have lied about over time and will try to distance themselves from you as much as possible. This is basically going to take away any kind of chance you have to manipulate them now or in the future.

The second issue that you are going to have is when the target sees that you are manipulating, it is going to shed some more light on what you were trying to do. This means that even if you were to try a new kind of tactic for persuasion or manipulation in the future, it is likely they are going to notice it. This is because they no longer trust you, and they are going to start putting all the actions that you do under a microscope to see what adds up and what doesn't.

This means that if you want to be as successful as possible with the process of manipulation, you have to be good at staying secretive about your intentions throughout the whole process. To do this, you need to take things slowly and make sure that you are picking out the right kind of target to work on for all of your needs.

Manipulation is a practice that you can technically use on anyone. There is not going to be any kind of limitation or restriction on who is able to use these techniques, or even when they are able to use them. Of course, most people will also make sure that they are not using the techniques of manipulation when it is seen as something illegal or when it is considered morally wrong. For example, most of the time it is frowned upon to manipulate another person into a relationship with you when it is against their will.

However, these strategies are going to be great to use in situations like negotiations with business because it helps you to make sure that you are getting what you want, helps you to change up the perception that the other person has of you, and other similar manners. There are some people who will use these techniques in the wrong manner and will use the techniques to get what they want, whether it is seen as illegal and unethical or not.

It is so important that if we want to be able to see some success with persuasion or manipulation or anything else that we are doing, that we are able to remain secretive, at least a little bit. We may be able to get away with the analysis and not being as tricky and sneaky as the others because people are always analyzing each other in our modern world. But if you don't be careful with the way that you are using the techniques that come with manipulation and persuasion, then the other person is going to catch on, and you are going to end up in a world of trouble then.

If you are worried about giving yourself away, or if you have had a few close calls that could have derailed the whole thing, this means that you are going through the process too fast. It is much better to take things slow and work through them, forming a good connection with the other person and really getting them to feel like they know you and trust you, rather than just jumping in and hoping that it is all going to work out.

The moment that the other person, the moment that your target, realizes what you are doing against them, and they find out that you are going to use persuasion and manipulation against them for your own benefit, then they are going to want to have nothing to do with you, they may tell others, and you are going to be exposed for all that you are trying to do against them.

It is much better to take your time, do a good analysis, and then pick the technique that you want to use and get them on your side ahead of time. it may take a bit longer, but you will find that this method is much more effective in the long run.

Subconscious Techniques for Persuasion

Persuasiveness is an effective aptitude everybody ought to learn. It is helpful in incalculable circumstances. For both your business and your personal life, being inspiring and influential to others will be the foundation for accomplishing objectives and being successful.

Learning about the traps of persuasion will give you

new awareness for when they appear in sales messaging you read. The greatest advantage? Your cash stays in your pocket. It literally pays for you to understand exactly how sales representatives and marketers offer you items that you don't really require. The following are some persuasive techniques that work on a subconscious level.

Outlining Impacts Thought

Let's say you're thirsty, and someone hands you a glass of water not-quite full. "The glass is half full." An optimist would "outline" the reality of your glass of water in that way. Outlining is used as an approach to modify how we classify, connect, and attach meaning to every aspect of our lives.

The headline "FBI Operators Surround Cult Leader's Compound" creates a mental picture strikingly different from another version of the headline for the same story: "FBI Specialists Raid Small Christian Gathering of Women and Children." Both headlines may convey what happened, however, the selected words affect the readers' mental and emotional responses, and therefore direct the impact the target events have on the article's readers.

Outlining is employed by apt government representatives. For example, representatives on both sides of the abortion debate refer to their positions as "pro-choice" or "pro-life." This is intentional, as "pro" has a more positive association to build arguments on. Outlining an event, product, or service this way unobtrusively utilizes emotional words strategically to persuade individuals to see or accept your perspective.

Creating a convincing message is as easy as selecting words that summon strategic pictures in the minds of your audience. Indeed, even with neutral words surrounding it, a solitary stimulating word can be powerful.

Reflecting as Persuasive Strategy

Reflecting, often called "the chameleon effect," is the act of replicating the movements and non-verbal communication of the individual you want to persuade. By mirroring the actions of the individual listening, you create an appearance of empathy.

Hand and arm motions, inclining forward or reclining away, or different head and shoulder movements are types of non-verbal communication you can reflect.

We, as a whole, do this without much thought, and now that you're becoming aware of that, you'll notice not only yourself but others doing it, as well.

It is important to be graceful, thoughtful about it and allow just a couple seconds to pass between their movements and you reflecting them.

Highlight Scarcity of a Product or Service

The concept of scarcity is often employed by marketers to make products, services, or associated events and deals appear to be all the more engaging on the grounds that there will be restricted accessibility. The belief is that there is a huge amount of interest for it if availability is scarce. For example, an ad for a new product might say: Get one now! They're selling out quickly!

Again, it literally pays to know that this is a persuasion strategy that you will see everywhere. Consider this concept the next time you settle on your buying choice. This principle triggers a feeling of urgency in most individuals, so it is best used when applied in your marketing and sales copy.

Reciprocity Helps Make a Future Commitment

When somebody helps us out, we feel responsible to provide a proportional payback. All in all, the next time you need someone to accomplish something beneficial for you, consider doing something unexpectedly pleasant for them first.

At work, you could pass a colleague a lead. At home, you could offer to loan some landscaping tools to a neighbor.

The details, where or when you do it, won't make a difference; the key is to supplement the relationship without being sought out first. Lead with value and give it freely, without overtly expecting anything in return, and their response will come.

Timing Can Bolster Your Good Fortune

Individuals will be more pleasant and accommodating when they're mentally exhausted. Before you approach somebody for something they may not otherwise participate in, consider holding back until they've recently accomplished something mentally challenging. Consider making your offer toward the end of the work day, for example, when you can get a colleague or

111

collaborator on the way out of the office. Whatever you may ask, a reasonable reaction could be, "I'll deal with it tomorrow."

Enhance Compliance to Acquire a Needed Result

To avoid cognitive dissonance, we all try to be true to how we've acted in the past. A reliable technique business people use is to shake your hand as they are consulting with you. We have been taught that a handshake equals a "sealed deal," and by doing this before the arrangement is really sealed, the business person has taken a step to persuade you into believing the deal is already done.

One approach to employing this yourself is influencing individuals to act before their minds are made up. Let's say that you are roaming downtown with a companion, and you decide you want to go see a movie at the local theater; yet, your companion is undecided. Compliance can come into play if you begin strolling toward the theater while they are still thinking about it. Your companion will probably consent to go once they realize you are strolling in the theater's direction.

Attempt Fluid Discourse

In the natural flow of our speech, interjections and reluctant expressions act as fillers when we need a moment to think or select the "right" word, for example, "um" or "I mean," and obviously the newly pervasive "like." These fillers have the unintended impact of making us appear to be unsure and doubtful and, in this way, less convincing. When you're certain about your message, others will be more effectively persuaded.

If you have trouble finding the right words at the right time, practice some free-flow association every day in front of the mirror for 60 seconds. You can add it to your morning ritual, or you can do it while having a shower, like I usually do. Basically, your goal in these 60 seconds is to jump from one topic to another very quickly, by associating words; do your best to avoid "um," "like," or other fillers.

Example: The water on my back right now is so hot, it reminds me of the hot weather in California. I love Cali; I like the food there. Mexican food is so spicy and hot, like Mexican women. I remember Marcella, that one Mexican girl I met last time I was there; she was probably the only blonde girl from Mexico. She was blonde like a Swedish model. I've never been to

Sweden, but I've heard it's cold out there...

And so on, until you get to 60 seconds without pauses or interjections. Once you reach that point after some practice, you can aim for 120 seconds. Once you've done that, the next step is to practice this game with other people. You don't need to go on for a full two minutes straight, but while you're talking to someone, you can go on a tangent for 20 seconds and practice the free-flow association skill. You'll practice and improve tremendously, while they'll be wondering "This guy is interesting. I really want to know what he's going to say next..."

Group Affinity Can Affect Decisions

We always seek the people around us to help us make decisions; people have an inherent need for belonging and acknowledgment, as previously discussed. We have a much higher tendency to imitate or be persuaded by somebody we like or by somebody we see as an influential leader.

A compelling approach to make this work for you, bolstering your good fortune, is to be viewed as a leader by your target audience—regardless of whether you officially have the title. It helps to be enchanting and sure, so individuals will have more confidence in your message. Keep improving yourself, and you'll soon become more magnetic than everyone else.

If you're interacting with an individual who doesn't consider you to be a powerful person (for example, a rival at work or your irritating in-laws), you can, in any case, exploit group affinity. For example, if you praise a leader that individual respects, that praise then activates the positive associations in that individual's brain about that admired leader, which creates a mental space where they can relate those qualities with you.

Create a Photo Opportunity with Man's Best Friend

Give your target audience the idea that you're trustworthy, and motivate them to be loyal to you, by taking a photo of yourself with a pooch (it doesn't need to be your own puppy). This can make you appear kind and cooperative, but keep these kinds of photo-ops to a minimum; setting up an excessive number of pictures looks amateurish. On a side note, it pays to know your audience; if you know they share a lot of cat pictures, maybe try a picture or two with a feline friend, too.

Offer a Drink

This might seem too easy, but giving the individual you want to persuade a warm drink to hold while you're conversing with them can be persuasive in itself. The warm vibe you've offered their hands (and their body) can intuitively make them see you as candidly warm, affable, and inviting. Offering a chilly drink can do the opposite! As a rule, individuals tend to feel "frosty" and seek out warm beverages when they're feeling stressed or overwhelmed, so take care of that need keeping in mind the end goal to make them more open.

Start with a Simple "Yes" Question

Start the discussion with an inquiry that creates a "Yes" reaction. "Nice weather we're having, isn't it?" or "You're searching for a great price on a car, right?"

When you get somebody saying yes, it's anything but difficult to motivate them to proceed, up to and including "Yes, I'll get it." You can counter this in your daily life by giving cautious answers to even the simplest questions.

Gently Break the Contact Boundary

You could be sealing a deal or asking somebody out for coffee, and touching them (in a modest and suitable way) can enhance your odds of hearing "Yes," because you have intuitively triggered the human yearning to connect.

In a professional setting, it is normally best to "touch" verbally by giving consolation or acclaim, as a physical touch could be seen as lewd behavior.

In sentimental circumstances, any delicate touch from a lady will more often than not be taken well. Men will need to proceed here with extreme caution—keeping in mind the end goal is to abstain from making a lady feel uncomfortable.

UNDERSTANDING DECEPTION

Once manipulation is identified, the next step is to get through it. Overcoming manipulation can be very challenging. In some cases, a 60 year-old-man might realize just now that his 85 year-old-mother is manipulative. They might never get through their issues, but they should still be confronted. Manipulation takes a part of both the abuser and the victim. It can ruin people's lives, altering the direction they take and affecting the rest of their years. Manipulation can be hard to identify and even harder to overcome.

It can be done, and it should be attempted to get through. In a relationship based around manipulation, there might not be any coming back. Sometimes, people might just have to break up. You might have to get a divorce or stop calling your mom. It takes two people to partake in a manipulative scenario. Not both people will end up identifying it as a manipulative situation, however. In that case, the person that realizes what's actually going on might just have to move on, the manipulator never realizing the damage they caused.

This can be a challenging part of overcoming manipulation. Usually, some instance of codependency formed, making it even harder to break away. There are ways to overcome this, and we will cover that in the next few sections.

Know Your Worth

The first step in overcoming manipulation is for the victim to identify that they still have value. A manipulator likely took everything from their victim. They belittled them, ridiculed them, and made them feel as though what they thought didn't matter. In some situations, they might have even used gaslighting tactics to make their victims feel as though they're insane. It can be hard for a victim to then recognize just how much value they still have once they become aware of the manipulation.

It's important for everyone to know, no matter who is reading this, that you have worth. Everyone has value. No one deserves to be manipulated. No one deserves to feel as though they don't have any purpose, reason, or value. You have the right to be treated justly, and with respect from other people. You are allowed to express your emotions, feelings, wants, and opinions. No one else has the right to tell you how to feel. You set your own boundaries, and no one else gets to decide for you.

If you feel sad about something, that is completely valid. No one gets to decide if what they say hurts you or not. Not everyone might intentionally mean to hurt you, but that doesn't mean you're not allowed to still feel bad. You have the right to feel the way you do, and you have the same right to express those beliefs.

If you feel like you need to protect yourself, you are just in doing so. If you feel like your safety is being threatened, or someone is taking advantage of you, you have the right to remove yourself from that situation without guilt. No one gets to treat you badly, and though that can be hard for many of us to hear, it's the truth.

Manipulators aim to take these thoughts away. They want to deprive their victims of their rights in order to work towards getting what they want. This can't happen anymore. It's up to the manipulator's victims to now recognize their worth and stop the cycle of manipulation.

Don't Be Afraid to Keep Your Distance

Many people that feel as though they're being manipulated end up being too afraid to do anything about it. They have been stripped of their own thoughts and opinions, their own feelings invalidated and instead focus on how other people feel. Those that have been continually manipulated might be afraid to leave those that have hurt them. They've depended on those that abused them for so long they don't know where else to go.

You're allowed to keep your distance. You don't have to feel guilty about protecting yourself. It can be hard to separate yourself from a manipulator, especially in a romantic relationship. You might see the very weaknesses that cause their manipulative behavior. Maybe in a relationship, a boyfriend's dad was an abusive alcoholic, and it greatly hurt him. It also caused his violent manipulative behavior that led him to hitting his girlfriend on a few occasions. It's true that he has his own pain, but that doesn't mean he's allowed to inflict it on others. The girlfriend has every right to leave her boyfriend and find her own peace and protection.

Ask what is really lost by leaving the person that's manipulating you. More often than not, value in a relationship is placed on codependent tendencies. A person is afraid to leave not because they love their manipulator, but because they are afraid to be alone. It can be scary to be on your own, but mostly because manipulators put that idea in their victims in the first place. Manipulators will trick their victims into staying with them because deep down, they know that the victim will be just fine without them.

It's Not Your Job to Change Them

Once manipulation is recognized, the next step is to try to talk to the person about the manipulation. It's time to get down to the root issues of the relationship and figure out what can be done to help both partners get what they need, instead of just the manipulator. There has been an imbalance of power for far too long, and it's time to rebalance.

Unfortunately, not many manipulators are willing to admit their faults and later change their behavior. Instead, they'll do whatever they can to distract others from their faults, placing the blame on their victims instead. When this happens, the victim has to accept that their manipulator isn't going to change, and they must find the strength to leave.

There will likely be a desire to change the other person and help them improve their life as well. Not everyone will always be on the same page of their journey towards self-discovery. It can be hard to accept for some victims, but they have to realize that it's not their job to change their manipulator.

You can only help a person so much, and if they're not willing to change or improve themselves, it's not going to happen. Many people wait around for the other to change in their relationship, hoping their manipulation will get better. If a person isn't aware of their behavior and aren't actively trying to change it, nothing is going to happen in the end.

Hypnosis

If mind control is the best set of manipulation strategies for beginners to pick up and be able to learn quickly, then hypnosis is the next natural step in the process towards becoming a master of manipulation.

In general, hypnosis lasts longer and is far more powerful than mind control is, although it also requires more skill to successfully pull off. While hypnosis has some concepts that overlap with mind control and brainwashing, it also has completely unique components, which can make it more challenging to learn. Hypnosis has a long a rich history, and today it is used in a wide variety of fields and industries, including in medicine, sports, psychotherapy, self-improvement, meditation and relaxation, forensics and criminal justice, art and literature, and the military. Of course, all instances of hypnosis share common characteristics no matter what context it is used in, and these same characteristics can come in handy when attempting to manipulate someone else. Having a good understanding of the principles and concepts of hypnosis can turn you from a mediocre manipulator into a highly skilled one.

The Hypnotic Trance

At its core, hypnosis is all about planting ideas into somebody else's subconsciousness in order to influence their consciousness. If you manage to infiltrate a person's subconsciousness with enough skill, they will not be aware of what you are doing, and will never know that you ever influenced them at all. The best way to access someone's subconsciousness is to coax them into a relaxed, meditative state known as a hypnotic trance. Getting your target into a trance is the most difficult part of the process of hypnosis, but once you finally manage to pull it off, you will have a much easier time successfully manipulating them. Putting your target into a trance allows for you to have direct access to their subconsciousness, as their consciousness will no longer be an active part of their mind for the duration of the trance. The trace is what separates hypnosis from mind control, and the ability to induce it in somebody else is what separates a beginner of manipulation from a budding expert.

The best way to think of a hypnotic trance is a form of deep relaxation. You are likely already familiar with the overall concept of the trace, due to portrayals of hypnosis in book, movies, and popular culture in general. Of course, in real life, you cannot put somebody else into a hypnotic trance simply by waving a watch in front of their face or by using a magical code phrase that will put them to sleep. Instead, putting someone into a hypnotic trance takes lots of time and skill, and it may not always work on every single person that you try it out on, especially when you are first starting to attempt to use it. In fact, for the best introduction to the hypnotic trance, you may want to find a friend who is willing to allow you to put them into a trance in order to practice doing it, or if you cannot find someone who is a willing participant, you can always put yourself into a hypnotic trance using this same method. If you fail at putting somebody into a trance, you are likely to face a negative reaction from that person, as they are likely to recognize suspicious behavior when they see it if they still have full awareness of their surroundings. This is why it is important that you practice this technique several times before attempting it on any outsiders, as you are far more likely to succeed in putting somebody into a hypnotic trance if you have some familiarity with how it already works.

The first step in putting your target into a hypnotic trance is to make sure that they are in a sitting position, or even better, lying down. After all, once your target is in the trance and their consciousness has temporarily faded away, they will no longer physically be able to stand up or support the weight of their own body. An action as forceful and abrupt as falling on the floor will be enough to wake them up from the hypnotic trance, and once they have regained their awareness, they will likely want an explanation as to what happened. Obviously, this is not a situation that you want to be caught in, so it is important to make sure that your target's body is in a secure position that will not fall over or cause them to wake up once you have put them in the trance. This also means that you should not attempt to hypnotize anybody unless there is a couch, chairs, a bed, or another piece of comfortable furniture for your target to use. Convincing your target to sit or lay down sounds more difficult than it actually is. Remember that your target will be more likely to sit or lay down if a piece of furniture is offered to them to do so on and that you should be prepared to sit or lay down first, as your target will be more likely to do the same if they are following your lead. If all else fails, you can always mind control them and influence them to sit or lay down where you want them to. Do not worry too much about how you make your target get into the best position and instead focus your attention on what comes after you have already convinced them to do so.

The next step in the process of putting someone into a hypnotic trance is to get your target to listen to the sound of your voice. In hypnotic techniques, your voice can be a powerful tool as long as you know how to use it correctly. Take special note of the fact that this step does not instruct you to start a conversation with your target, but rather to get them to listen to you. This is because when attempting to put another person into a hypnotic trance, your voice is not being used to express any meaning or to describe any information, but rather as a way to create a sort of white noise, which will allow your target to slip further and further into a deeply relaxed state. If your target is engaged by what you are saying and tries to respond, then they are not letting go of their awareness, and their consciousness is still very much active. When attempting to put your target in a hypnotic trance, when you are first beginning to speak to them, the content of what you are saying matters a tremendous amount. You need to choose a topic that is interesting enough for them to want to stick around and listen to, but not so interesting that they are completely engrossed in what you are saying and are trying to speak back to you. The topic that you choose is likely to vary from target to target, as everyone has different tastes as to what kind of subject they are willing to pay attention to or not. This is where skills learned under controlling the narrative can come in handy; if you are able to tell a long, meandering story instead of a short and sweet one, especially about something that your target does not particularly care about, then they should begin falling into a hypnotic trance relatively easily. When you are speaking, be sure to use a calm, soothing voice, and choose words and phrases to use that are generally simple and easy to understand. This allows your target to focus on the overall sound of your voice, rather than what exactly you are saying. However, if you make your voice sound too calm and soothing, your target may think that something is wrong with you or may grow suspicious of your intentions. Therefore, try not to sound too much like a guided meditation instructor and instead attempt to model your voice in the style of the narrator of a nature documentary. Keep in mind that your goal is to relax your target, but not to put them to sleep. If you make yourself sound too soothing, you will run the risk of having your target be too relaxed. If your target is asleep, after all, they will not be open to any suggestions that you make, as they will be unconscious. Once you see that your target has fallen into a more and more relaxed state, the content of what you are saying to them will not matter as much, and as long as you keep your voice in a steady, soothing tone, you will not have to worry about what topic you are speaking about any longer.

Advanced Techniques and Suggestibility Testing

At this point we have learned about various methods of manipulation through neuro-linguistic programming and hypnosis. By now you are armed with a plethora of weapons to use on any given subject, and you are prepared defensively if someone attempts to use any of these tactics against you. In this chapter, we will go over a couple of new topics that aren't manipulation tactics in and of themselves – they are nonetheless crucial for knowing upon whom to deploy these tactics on and for the defense of the manipulator.

Suggestibility Testing

Many hypnotists will tell you that suggestibility testing is best left to the street performers and entertainment hypnotists. This may be true as it has limited viability in hypnotherapy but what many hypnotists don't think about is everyday manipulation. Suggestibility testing is vastly utilizable in the realm of conversational hypnosis and everyday hypnosis towards the ends of manipulation. So what it is?

Suggestibility testing can refer to any number of verbal or physical "feelers" that help the hypnotist determine whether or not their subject is a good target for hypnosis and manipulation. They can serve as a guide for one to determine how likely a subject will bend to their will. Some hypnotists use suggestibility training to determine how deep into a hypnotic trance their subjects are but our purposes will be a little different.

For our intents and purposes we will use suggestibility testing to find our subjects in the first place. The reason anyone would want to use suggestibility testing is to find the right subject for manipulation. The caveat with hypnotism, even conversational hypnosis, is that some people are more suggestible to others. In other words, some people are less likely to be inducted into hypnosis than others. For this reason Dark NLP practitioners often use suggestibility testing to have a better idea of who they can manipulate and who they might not be able to.

The reason you will want to learn these tests is essentially for efficiency. For example, you wouldn't want to use a lot of your time and effort trying to manipulate someone whom you've tested to have low suggestibility. It would just take too long and besides, there are tons of easily suggestible targets to choose from. In fact, it is estimated that as much as 80% of the population is in the average range of hypnotic suggestibility – meaning that up to 80% of the population can be successfully hypnotized with moderate effort.

That is why suggestibility testing is so useful for the Dark NLP practitioner. It gives a good guideline on who a prime subject might be and helps the practitioner avoid difficult subjects.

Suggestibility tests can be deployed fairly easily. In most cases you should try at least one of these tests before you try using any of the tactics we have discussed so far. Let's take a look at some of the best methods for testing suggestibility.

The Light/Heavy Hands Technique

This method of suggestibility testing depends heavily on the concentration and that imagination of the subject. How keenly a person can bring their concentration and imagination into alignment is a very important factor. It will determine how susceptible they will be to actual hypnotic suggestion.

In this test you will be able to see a physical manifestation of their level of suggestion. It is sometimes called the book and balloon test as well and you will see why in just a moment. The idea behind this test is to see just how deeply one can delve into their own minds. The belief is that the body will react physically if someone is concentrating on something that they believe is true. If you see that your subject reacts bodily to the light/heavy hands technique then they are more than likely a prime target for Dark NLP and hypnosis. So here is what you are going to want to do:

Ask someone, or multiple people, to close their eyes and hold their arms straight out in front of them. Tell them to have one hand turned palm-up to the sky and one hand palm-down to the ground. Now tell them to imagine that in the hand that is facing toward the sky, they are carrying a watermelon. In the hand they have facing the ground, tell them that there are a bunch of helium balloons tied to their wrist.

Go into detail about the watermelon. They can smell it, feel its rind and most importantly, feel how heavy it is. With each passing moment their arms are getting more and more fatigued from the weight of the heavy watermelon. Meanwhile the arm with the balloons tied to it is getting lighter as the balloons are slowly and gently ascending towards the sky. What you should be doing while their eyes are closed is seeing if their arms are actually moving. If they are, then you've most likely found your subject.

The Amnesia Technique

The amnesia technique is a verbal test. In it you will ask the potential subject to forget about something for a period of time (it shouldn't be more than a few minutes). For example, you can ask your subject to forget the letter P. Tell them to pretend that the letter P never existed and to forget that you even told them to forget about it. Then ask them to recite the alphabet. People who are moderately or highly suggestible will skip over the letter P (or whatever letter you tell them to forget) and not even realize it. Once again, if the person you tried this test on skips over the letter you told them to forget, they may be a good subject to zone in on.

The Locked Hand Technique

The locked hand technique (also known as the hand clasp technique) is another physical test that the subject will have to be willing to participate in. Like the light/heavy hand technique, it will test just how deeply a person can concentrate on the words you are saying to them and what you are telling them to imagine. Ask your subject to clap their hands together and keep them together, palm to palm. Then tell them to interlace their fingers. Make sure that you maintain fixed eye-contact with them throughout this test and tell them to push their hands together as tightly as they can. Tell them to imagine their hands merging into one piece of solid flesh and bone. After a minute or two, tell them to stop pushing and try pulling their hands apart. Again, a potential manipulation subject will find it hard to pull their hands away from each other.

SPEED READING PEOPLE

What Is Speeding People?

Ignite the Art of Reading People through Your Super Senses

If you want to read people, you have to don the garment of a psychiatrist who has the power to interpret cues which are verbal and nonverbal. You need to observe beyond people's masks into their real self. You may not get the entire picture about anybody through logic alone. You have to surrender to their critical forms of information to interpret the essential nonverbal perceptive cues that individuals exude. For you to achieve this feat, you need to be eager to surrender emotional baggage like ego clashes or old resentments and also any preconceptions which can prevent you from making out the person. It is crucial, as well, for you to obtain information without bias and continue to be impartial without twisting it.

In the process of reading a colleague, your boss, or partner for you to understand them accurately, some walls need to come down, and you need to surrender biases. You need to be ready to let go of limiting, old ideas as far as intellect is concerned. Those who read other people well are taught to comprehend the hidden. They have discovered how they will draw on what is called 'super-sense' so they can take a profound observation beyond where you usually steer your focus when you attempt to hack into transformative awareness.

Examine cues of body language

When you are reading the cues of body language, you have to surrender the focus by releasing your struggle to understand the hidden signals of body language. Never get analytical or overtly intense. Stay fluid and relaxed. Observe by sitting back comfortably.

Focus on appearance

When you are reading other people, take note of what they are wearing. Are they putting on well-shined shoes and power suit? The indication for success is when someone deck out decently. For someone wearing a T-shirt and jeans may be an indicator of that person being comfortable with casual. It may be a signal of a seductive choice when someone wears a tight top with cleavage. A pendant like Buddha or cross may indicate spiritual values.

Notice posture

Postures are an essential aspect of reading people. It's a sign of confident when people's head is held high. Or you can get an indication of low self-esteem when they cower, or they walk irresolutely. You can also get a sign of a big ego when they have puffed-out chest and swagger.

Pay attention to physical movements

When you read others, look out for their distance and learning. In general, people bend forward at those they like and keep a distance from others they don't. Also, when people cross their arms and legs, you can see signs of anger, self-protection, or defensiveness. It is an indication that people are hiding something when they hide their hands by placing them in their pockets, laps, or place them behind them. With cuticle picking or lip biting, you will get a sign of people attempting to calm themselves in a difficult circumstance or under pressure.

Read facial expression

Our faces provide the outline for our emotions. Profound frown lines indicate over-thinking or worry. The smile lines of delight are crow's feet; pursed lips is a signal of contempt, anger, or bitterness. While teeth grinding and clenched jaw are indicators of tension.

Take note to your intuition

It is possible to tune into someone ahead of their words and body language. Though not what your head says, what your gut feels is intuition. Instead of logic, intuition is your perception of nonverbal information through images. If you are in the process of understanding a person, their outer trappings are insignificant, and it is only who the person is what counts. To reveal a richer story, intuition gives the power to distinguish beyond the obvious to tell a richer story.

You need to watch out for these checklists cues of intuition:

Respect your gut feelings

Pay attention to voices of your gut, in particular when

connecting with someone for the first time, an automatic rejoinder that happens out of impulse. Gut feelings are as a result of if you are tensed up or at ease. As a cardinal response, gut feelings occur in an instant. They are meters of your inner truth that relay to you if you should trust someone.

Goosebumps feelings

Pleasant, intuitive shivers are goosebumps, and they happen when something strikes a chord in us in connection with our resonance to individuals that inspire or move us. Also, goosebumps occur in the course of going through déjà-vu and when you have never met someone before but still recognize them.

Listen to sparkles of insight

During a conversation with people, you may be impressed by those who come quickly. Watch out and stay alert. Or else, you might fail to spot it. For most of us, this crucial awareness is lost because of the inclination to move onto the next idea.

Look for insightful empathy

This cue happens when you have a passionate type of

empathy through the feelings of someone's real emotions and symptoms within your body. So, while reading people, take note whether you had pain on your back when it wasn't there before, or if you are upset or depressed following a mind-numbing conference. To determine if empathy is at play, get feedback.

Discern emotional power

The vibe we radiate and the remarkable demonstration of our energy are emotions. It is with an intuition that we procure these emotions. For some people, you will be happy to be around them because they enhance your vitality and mood. Others tend to be draining; get away from them is what you want. Though it is undetectable, you can feel this 'subtle energy' feet or inches from the body. It's called **chi** in Chinese medicine, an essential healthy vitality.

Be aware of the presence of people

Though not substantially similar to our behavior or words, the accustomed energy we discharge is when we sense the presence of the people. It is typical of a rain cloud or the sun that borders around our emotional atmosphere. In the process of reading people, take note of if you get attraction with their presence or retreating due to the willies you are getting.

Watch people's eyes

Humans' eyes convey compelling forces. As the eyes cast off an electromagnetic signal, according to studies, the brain does the same. When you watch people's eyes, you will know if they are tranquil, sexy, mean, angry, or caring. Also, you will have the ability to determine if a person wants intimacy in their eyes or their eyes can give signs that they are comfortable. Even in their eyes, you will know whether they appear to be hiding or guarded.

Observe the feel of a hug, handshake, or touch

Most of us shake emotional energy, similar to an electrical flow during physical contact. You can ask yourself if a hug or handshake feel comfortable, warm, or confident. Or if it is repulsive so much that you wish to withdraw. You can know the sign of anxiety with someone's hand clammy or limp to suggest being timid or non-committal.

Listen to the tone of laugh and voice

Our voice's volume and tone are capable of telling a lot about our emotions. Vibration is as a result of sound frequencies. Notice how people's pitch of voice affects you in the course of reading them. Envisage if the tone is snippy, abrasive, and whiny or if their tone feels soothing.

To read people can be hard sometimes. It takes practice and courage. However, once you are past that, you will gain a significant advantage. Not only will you survive, but you will also thrive in all your relationships with others. People will approach you. Opportunities will come to you. And some people will want to be like you.

CONCLUSION

Thank you for making it through to the end. Let's hope it was informative and able to provide you with all of the tools you need to achieve your goals whatever they may be.

The next step is to be on the lookout for those who may try to use some of these techniques against you. If you are not on the lookout, a dark manipulator may be able to use these tactics against you, and you may never know.

Now that we have gone through a number of nonverbal cues, it is worth noting that there are some cues that you may never see due to cultural differences. For instance, close proximity is considered aggressive in Japan. Constant eye contact also makes people very uncomfortable, whereas in Spanish and Arabic cultures, NOT maintaining a lot of eye contact is considered very disrespectful. For the majority of the nonverbal cues here, however, you shouldn't have any problems, just be sure to do a little research if you like to travel, so that you don't misinterpret a cue if you intend to go somewhere exotic.

Now that we have given you a larger sampling of the information that you need you will want to practice it. You will find a number of them readily in the workplace and at social venues that you frequent. Use this information to better arm yourself for dealing with Dark Psychology. Arm yourself as best you can with this information. It's the good stuff!

If you have made it this far in the book, congratulations. You have learned some of the most powerful and useful tools for manipulation and NLP. You are now equipped with all the tools you will need to not only be aware of people trying to manipulate you, but also to get people to do what you want. There is only one more thing to do: develop a strong sense of self.

As you go over these techniques and learn about what it really means to influence others towards your own ends, it is easy to get lost in the concepts. You may start to feel like you have been manipulated yourself. You may feel that in order to deploy these techniques, you will have to start to believe in untruths.

This is not the case and following this train of thought can be very dangerous. It can lead you to forget who you really are and what you really believe. When you do that, you not only become a kind of aimless wanderer in life but you also become a prime target for manipulation yourself. This is why it is infinitely important to develop a strong mentality and sense of self. Doing so will keep you from losing your original intent and identity. It will also ensure that you are not made a puppet in someone else's marionette theater.

Victim Versus Manipulator

It is important to know how to use these powerful tactics responsibly. We are not condoning that you go out and try to scam every person you know. These tactics should be used sparingly and only when you really need them. They can be used responsibly to help yourself get out of a bad situation or relationship. They can be used responsibly when you are in dire need of help but have no one willing to lend a hand. They can be used responsibly by remembering always that the "subjects" you manipulate are people as well.

Speaking of "subjects," we have used this word a lot in this book but it is crucial to know the difference between subject and manipulator or victim and manipulator. The lines between these two concepts can be blurred in your mind without you even realizing. When that happens you are easy pickings. A skilled manipulator will be able to spot you from a mile away and take advantage. It becomes of chief importance to step out of the victim role and be aware of yourself and your surroundings so that you are not the victim of manipulation yourself.

This is the perfect time to take an honest look at yourself through the lens of all the topics and techniques that we have discussed in this book to see if you are being or have been manipulated in the past. Be fearless in your memory and introspection. Has anyone ever used these techniques on you? Is someone in your life using these techniques on you now?

Take responsibility for your actions. Even if you are realizing now that you have or are being manipulated, don't wallow in regret. Don't feel sorry or bad about yourself. Realize that everyone has been manipulated at least once in their lives. The important thing is that you realize it now and can now take the step toward shedding the role of the victim. When you remain in the victim mentality – thinking that you are "so dumb" for letting someone manipulate you or that you will only repeat these mistakes – you remain an easy target.

Stepping out of the victim role and into the role of the manipulator is your first step in solidifying your identity and steeling yourself mentally. Own up to how you have been used in the past and move on from it. Just because it happened once or twice or three or even hundreds of times does not mean that it has to keep happening. Start thinking of yourself as a manipulator every day. Distance yourself from victim thinking and take control. Look at yourself in the mirror every day and say to your reflection "I am in control." It may feel silly at first but it is an effective way to program yourself out of victim thinking.

Developing a strong mentality will make it much easier for you to impose your influence on someone else and keep other people from doing the same to you. It is what you must do if you want to become a skilled manipulator. Learning the techniques is not enough. Manipulation is a mental exercise and keeping a strong mind will make you more successful at this exercise. Stepping out of the victim role is just the first step. There is more you can do to fortify your mind and identity.

Meditation and Grounding

A strong mind is a grounded mind, but what does it mean to be mentally grounded? Being mentally grounded means that you have an unwavering point of reference to who you are at your core. Think of it like your own mental refuge to turn to when life gets too chaotic. In terms of manipulation, being mentally grounded will help center you from the lies that you may have to tell or the lies that you hear. It was stated earlier in this section that when practicing manipulation, it can be very easy to get lost or out of touch with your own reality.

That is where mental grounding comes into play. When you are mentally grounded you will never lose touch with your own reality and lose yourself in the many roles you may have to play when manipulating. It isn't always easy to find mental grounding though and it can be even more difficult to maintain. Before we get into ways you can become more mentally grounded, be aware that this is not a one-and-done practice. However you find best to mentally ground yourself should become a regular if not every day routine for you. Think of your mind like a car. When you manipulate, or even when you are just out in the world and interacting with others, you are putting miles on your mind. Every once in awhile, you need to change the oil and tune it up. For as long as you have a brain, you need to practice regular mental grounding.

So let's look at some ways to achieve a grounded mind:

- Meditation – Meditation is the practice of clearing your mind and focusing on your breathing. This is very difficult to do at first but the more you practice it, the better you will get at it and the more you will benefit from it. Try finding a quiet little spot where you can sit down on the ground or lay. This should be somewhere you will not be disturbed. Start with just 20 minutes a day in which you come to rest in this place, close your eyes, try to clear your mind and focus only on your breathing pattern. Focus solely on maintaining a uniform breathing pattern. When you feel more comfortable doing this for 20 minutes, increase it to ten more minutes and on and on in that fashion.

- Being Amongst Nature – There is a Buddhist parable called "The Sermon of the Inanimate." In this parable, a practitioner sat quietly in a forest and observed the nature around him; the trees, the grass, the rocks etc. He found that inanimate nature, by merit of being still has a lot to teach us. Being amongst nature is a good way to find your mental grounding. It doesn't have to be a forest. It could be a small park in your neighborhood. Just as long as you are more or less surrounded by natural things. Spend time here regularly and you will come to find that the needs and concerns of society are not the same as the needs and concerns of nature. The trees are not stressed about work. The rocks don't care about material matters like cars and clothes. Unfortunately we cannot be in this state of bare tranquility all the time but finding your own nature refuge can go a long way towards re-centering and refocusing on what is important and real in your life.

- Take Night Walks – Have you ever noticed that when you walk you think a bit clearer? Maybe you have taken a walk with someone and found that you have more to talk about while walking. There is a reason for that. When our bodies are active our blood is flowing more which means more blood flow to the brain. Try taking a walk at night when you know there won't be a lot of cars or other people on the street. Think about your day and your interactions. Evaluate them beyond the surface encounters and compare them to what you believe and feel. This just might help you get to the hearts of various matters better and realize where your grounding lies.

Practice Improving Your Frame Control

Mental grounding helps a lot in maintaining your frame because your frame is what you truly believe to be true and what you care about in life. You cannot maintain your frame without first finding your mental grounding. That is why it is important to practice grounding as often as possible. When you constantly remind yourself of your beliefs it will be that much easier to maintain your frame.

A strong frame is all about not wavering under criticism and pressure. You will be challenged a lot, especially when you are using any of the tactics you have learned in this book. Under this pressure you must be confident that what you believe is right and true. You can use any of the tips we have discussed for increasing charisma and confidence like standing/sitting up straight, speaking deliberately and maintaining intent eye-contact. Increasing your level of confidence will help you build a song self-frame.

Use these techniques and practices with patience, perseverance, care and awareness. Remember always that having a strong mind is the first step toward being able to sway anybody. Know that the only way to protect yourself from other manipulators is to have a strong mind. Keep in touch with your sense of self at all times. If you do all of these things and take to heart all of the techniques and tactics that you have learned in this book, you will find your definition of success in psychological wisdom and understanding.

The goal of this book is to keep you out on the lookout for the dark manipulators who may show up in your life. When you know some of the signs to watch out for, and you understand dark psychology, you can protect yourself and stay safe! You are the one who should be in control of your own mind. Don't let someone else take that away from you!

ANALYZE PEOPLE

How To Analyze People Guide. Discover
The Secrets And Techniques Of Manipulation
For Mind Control And Persuasion. Speed
Reading Their Body Language And Behavior.

engaging in the rendering of legal, financial, medical or professional advice. The content within this book has been derived from various sources. Please consult a licensed professional before attempting any techniques outlined in this book.

By reading this document, the reader agrees that under no circumstances is the author responsible for any losses, direct or indirect, which are incurred as a result of the use of information contained within this document, including, but not limited to, — errors, omissions, or inaccuracies.

INTRODUCTION

Much of basic common body language is the same all over the world despite religion and racial differences. Some examples of this are smiling when you're happy or scowling when you are sad or angry. The nodding of the head is almost completely universally used to indicate an affirmation of sorts. It is believed that this form of affirmation is a genetic predisposition because individuals who were born blind still use this form of body language even though they never learned to use it visually.

This then brings me to an interesting point about body language and whether it is a learned action or genetic action. This is a debate that is ongoing and is still being researched even up to this day. Some forms of body language can be traced back to animal ancestry and are believed to be purely genetic. This is the action of sneering at another person in anger or irritation. An animal's a similar action to this is done when preparing for an attack.

There are three basic rules for an accurate reading of

somebody's body language. You must keep these three rules in mind when attempting to analyze any person for their body language.

1. Reading Clusters of Gestures Rather Than an Individual

You should never try to analyze or interpret a single solitary gesture separately from all of the others. You have to look at the entire picture. This means that you have to look at every action of the person's body and compare it to the rest of them. It is easy to remember this rule when you think of body language as just that: a language. As with any vocally spoken language, body language has its own "words," "sentences," and "punctuation." Attempting to understand somebody's body language through one specific gesture is like attempting to understand an entire paragraph from just a single word. You have to read each individual gesture as its own word and put them together to create sentences so that you can understand the language that someone's body is giving off. A common rule of thumb for this is the idea that someone needs at least three words to be able to create a proper sentence. As for body language, this means that you have to be able to compare at least three gestures that a person is giving off before you can begin to understand their innermost feelings and thoughts.

3. Searching for Consistency

This is especially important when trying to decide if somebody may be lying to you or not. Consistency is key in being able to tell if somebody is telling the truth. You have to consider the words that are coming out of their mouth in relation to what their body language is showing you. If an individual's words and body language are in conflict in a given moment, it is often best to ignore what is being said and focus instead on body language exclusively. Inconsistency between body language and vocal words is a strong sign of lying.

4. Context, Context, Context

Context is incredibly important when attempting to read a person's body language. You have to take into account an individual's environment, in addition to the signals that their body is giving off. There are lots of body symbols that have no meaning whatsoever when an individual is in certain situations. For instance, a person with arms and legs crossed tightly together on a cold winter's day is not necessarily a sign of feeling defensive—they are most likely just cold.

CHAPTER 1

WHY ANALYZE PEOPLE

Have you anytime looked at someone and thought you had them understood just from that look? Is it exact to state that you were right? Or then again would you say you were stirred up about some piece of their character? Despite whether you were right or wrong, you essentially tried getting someone, which is an ability that most of us would love to have. Everything considered, in case you can tell when your chief is feeling incredible, you understand when to demand a raise, right? When you understand your people are feeling awful you know, it is anything but a chance to unveil to them you scratched the vehicle. It is connected to appreciating what understanding people means and how it capacities.

The graph below shows the importance of nonverbal and verbal communication according to a survey conducted at the University of Michigan as of 2018.

What Is Reading People'?

When you look at someone and feel like you can condemn whether they are feeling extraordinary or a horrendous one, paying little heed to whether they are a wonderful individual or a mean one or whatever else using any and all means, you are getting them. At the point when all is said in done, understanding someone means researching them and it does not just should be a speedy look, and knowing something about them without them saying anything in any way shape or form. It is a tendency you get from looking and from viewing the way in which they stand, the way wherein they look around, the way where they move. There some different features that could play into your inclination and cognizance of them, yet the most critical thing is that they did not explicitly uncover to you whatever that thing is.

By and by, various people investigate someone and acknowledge they know something. You mull over inside 'charitable, they look sincere' or 'astonishing, they look upset.' These are instinctual suppositions and thoughts that we have when we see a person. As we speak with them, we may achieve new goals or even as we watch them over the room. Maybe you never banter with that individual, anyway you have examinations and considerations in regards to the kind of person that they rely upon what you have seen of them. You are getting them, and whether you are right or wrong is an assistant point.

For What Reason is Reading People Important?

For what reason would it be a smart thought for you to essentially disturb getting people? Everything considered, there are a couple of special reasons this can be a better than average capacity. In any case, at a most fundamental level, it reveals to you how you should approach someone. If they look neighborly, you might be also prepared to approach with a smile and a very much arranged welcome. If they look down and out, you might undoubtedly approach with a reason rather than basically stopping to make appropriate associate. If a friend looks upset, you may ask them what's going on or what happened. Understanding what they feel like just from a quick look can empower you to imagine whatever is going on essentially like that, and the better you get with the mastery, the better you'll be at talking with people.

In case you do not have the foggiest thought how to

scrutinize people in any way shape or form, you could wrap up interpreting something that they do or an action or an outward appearance mistakenly, and you may start to expect things about a person that is not correct. Maybe you see their face and accept that they are a perturbed person when they're basically furious with a condition. Maybe you think they look threatening, anyway they're basically perplexed with something that is going on around them. By making sense of how to scrutinize better, you'll have the alternative to push your life from numerous perspectives.

Understanding people can empower you to acknowledge who to approach with that unprecedented new idea (and when to approach) and who you ought to stay away from. It in like manner discloses to you how to familiarize something with them, paying little mind to whether from a precise perspective or dynamically fun and creative one. Before you know it, understanding people will be normal to you if you practice it routinely enough. Additionally, what's shockingly better is that you have no doubt been doing it for as long as you can remember and not despite contemplating it. That is in light of the fact that it is something that even kids will give a shot every so often, without acknowledging how huge it is.

Understanding People in Childhood

When you were an adolescent did you ever sit on a seat at the entertainment focus or on your porch and watch people walk around? You apparently did at some point or another, paying little mind to whether it was uniquely for a few minutes. Also, a short time later you look at the overall public and make stories. In the occasion that they're walking a canine, perhaps they're a pooch walker on their way to the entertainment focus. In the occasion that they're passing on an organizer case and walking quickly, they are late to a noteworthy social affair, clearly, that get-together may have been with outcasts in your young character, anyway, you get a general idea. You have successfully deciphered what you see of someone to make a story about them.

As you get progressively prepared, you use those proportional sorts of aptitudes to start understanding people extensively more and to some degree all the more accurately. Your cognizance of outward appearances and position start to develop to some degree more and before you know it you can look at someone and rapidly acknowledge what it is they are feeling at any rate, as a general rule. All things needed are a touch of producing for your childhood capacities and before you understand it you are en route to progressively significant accomplishment in your adult life.

Getting Help Reading People

Understanding people is a noteworthy ability to learn. For a large number of individuals, you probably look at is an 'acknowledge the main decision accessible' circumstance, is not that so? You accept on the off chance that I can scrutinize people, at that point extraordinary, yet if I cannot, well, no harm was done, is that not so? Everything considered, really understanding people energizes you a lot in your life and it causes you to be a prevalent individual as well, which is the reason it is a critical ability to have, paying little respect to whether you have a straightforward appreciation or an undeniably expansive one.

If you do not perceive how to examine people, it is a capacity that you irrefutably can learn. It is something that you can tackle for yourself by fundamentally coming back to those adolescent extensive stretches of making stories for the overall public walking around. And yet it is something that you can develop impressively further if you push yourself. The key is guaranteeing that you do not stop and do not desert the progression you are making. You may be bewildered precisely with the sum you can learn in a short proportion of time in case you move on these capacities, despite starting with people you certainly know.

For the people who are not sure where to start or how to wear down getting people, it is absolutely possible to get capable help with the strategy.

Starting with People You Know

It will, in general, be less complex to start scrutinizing the all-inclusive community you know before continuing forward to untouchables. These are people that you certainly know things about, and when you look at them, you can in all probability watch things that show those qualities. If your nearest friend is excessively bubbly and pleasant to everyone, you can undoubtedly look at them and jump on that trademark. Venture up to the plate and see them, see what it is about them that shows others they are bubbly and all around arranged and a while later quest for those characteristics in different people around you.

It moreover empowers us to move appropriately between our own one of a kind perspective and another. Unusually, social understanding relies upon information that cannot be truly observed at this point ought to be translated from moving toward information and our knowledge into the social world.

Moreover, continuously, confirmation proposes social cognizance incorporates reenactment, copying others' experiences as a way to deal with getting them. A real model here is the manner in which we experience other people's sentiments.

When watching someone's face we will, as a rule, duplicate her outward appearance, smiling when she does, glaring in comprehension. Such mimicry may not be obvious to the nice onlooker, yet minute muscle order can be distinguished in all regards not long in the wake of being exhibited to an energetic verbalization. Surely, even our eyes extend so as to the ones we are looking.

Research is beginning to exhibit this to be the circumstance.

Various people with mind hurt, oftentimes to the frontal folds of the cerebrum, develop excessively poor social aptitudes and social direct regardless of modestly incredible insight.

Basically, people with mental unevenness range issue seem to experience extraordinary difficulty with social information.

From a transformative perspective, it looks good that social discernment may have developed freely to non-social aptitudes.

Individuals are social animals relying upon interest and competition inside get-togethers to persevere. So the ability to see expressive motions and grasp the essentialness of social lead may be a transformative objective, realizing its improvement self-sufficiently of non-social information taking care of aptitudes.

Understanding the Brain

In some progressing work in my exploration office, we have found poor versatility and restriction can interfere with social understanding.

We requested a social event from adults who had persevered through genuine personality harm to finish a direct communication task: depict their "ideal" event resort. They were then drawn nearer to put themselves in the shoes of a substitute kind of event maker, for instance, a family with energetic adolescents.

When they had thought of their ideal inn, the speakers with mind harm could not delineate an event from someone else's perspective. Be that as it may, they did not have this issue when fundamentally gotten some data around two various types of event makers. The issue perhaps rose when self-contemplations were incited first.

Understanding social cognizance and how it might be exasperated in different kinds of mind issue holds remarkable certification for better assessment and remediation of social difficulties. It also assurances to open learning of how our cerebrums are wired to engage us to work in a social world.

More Imitation

Inside the mind itself, "reflect" neuron systems in the premotor cortex of the frontal projection are started when we watch the exercises of others. It creates the impression that we do not just reflect considerations, we furthermore reflect exercises!

Right when sound adults are set in fMRI scanners and got some data about the mental state of someone such as themselves, a comparative region of the prefrontal cortex is impelled as when they think about themselves. This additionally prescribes we appreciate others by reference to ourselves.

Facial mimicry can be blocked after mind harm notwithstanding the way that the reasons are still exploratory. If diversion clarifies social comprehension, there ought to be a type of control of the strategy so we are prepared to isolate between our very own experiences and that of others, and move between these adaptable.

CHAPTER 2

ANALYZING PERSONALITY PEOPLE

Personality analysis is a field that is constantly evolving and varied. There are varying schools of psychological thoughts and theories when it comes to studying an individual's personality. Some of the most popular personality analyzing schools include trait theory, social learning, biological/genetic personality influencer and more.

Personality refers to an individual's distinct characteristics connected to processing thoughts, feelings and emotions that eventually determine their behavior. It involves taking into consideration all the traits a person possess to understand them as an entity. Personality study also includes understanding the inherent differences existing between people where particular characteristics are concerned.

Here are some of the most common personality type classifications.

Type A, B, C and D

Type A personality people are at a bigger risk of contracting heart diseases since they are known to be more aggressive, competitive, ambitious, short-tempered, impatient, impulsive and hyper active. Type A personality theory was introduced in the 50's by Meyer Friedman and Ray Rosenman. These people are more stressed due to their constant need to accomplish a lot. They are always striving to be better than others, which invariably leads to greater anxiety and stress.

Type B people are more reflective, balanced, even-tempered, inventive and less competitive by personality. They experience less stress and anxiety, along with staying unaffected by competition or time constraints. A Type B personality person is moderately ambitious and lives more in the present. They have a steadier and more restrained disposition. Type B folks are social, modest, innovative, gentle mannered, relaxed and low on stress.

Later psychologists came up with other personality types, too, since they found the division into Type A and B more restrictive. They discovered that some people demonstrated a combination of both A and B Type traits. Thus, segregating people into only two distinct personality groups doesn't do justice to the classification. This lead to the creation of even more personality types!

Type C people have a more meticulous eye for detail. They are focused, curious and diplomatic. There tend to put other people's needs before theirs. They are seldom assertive, straightforward and opinionated. This leads to Type C folks developing pent up resentment, frustration, anxiety and depression. There is a propensity to take everything seriously, which makes them reliable and efficient workers.

This personality type also possess high analytic skills, logical thinking powers and intelligence. However, they need to develop the knack of learning to be less diplomatic and more assertive. Type C also needs to develop the ability to relax and let their hair down periodically.

Lastly, Type D personality people are known to hold a more pessimistic view of life. They are socially awkward and withdrawn, and do not enjoy being in the limelight. They are constantly worried about being rejected by people. Type D people are at a greater risk of suffering from mental illnesses such as depression owing to pessimism, pent up frustration and melancholy. Since the Type D personality doesn't share things easily with others, they suffer internally.

Psychoanalytic Theory

This theory is different from the regular personality classification theories in the sense that the analysis is based is not based on the responses of people about their personality, but a more in-depth study of people's personalities by glimpsing into their subconscious or unconscious mind. Since the analysis is based on a study on a person's subconscious mind, errors and instances of misleading the reader are eliminated.

In psychoanalysis, a person's words and actions are known to be disguised manifestations for their underlying subconscious emotions. The founding father of the psychoanalytic theory was Sigmund Freud, who was of the view that all human behavior is primarily driven by primitive instincts, passions, impulse and underlying emotions. He theorized that all human behavior is a direct consequence of the equation between our id, ego and superego.

Through the free association method that includes experiences, memories, dreams and more; Freud analyzed underlying emotions, thoughts and feelings that determine their attitude and behavior. Thus a majority of our behavior can be traced to our early childhood experiences that are still lingering in our subconscious mind, which we may or may not be aware of.

For example, if an individual demonstrates aggressive traits as an adult, it can be pinned down to the violence, harassment or bullying he/she experienced in their early childhood. Similarly, if a child comes from an environment where there were very high expectations from him/her and the parents were seldom happy with his/her accomplishments, he/she may constantly seek validation or acceptance from others. They may fear rejection.

Thus, a person's childhood experiences can help you determine their personality and read them even more effectively according to the psychoanalytic theory. The theory is still extensively used when it comes to helping people cope with depression, anger, stress, panic attacks, aggression, obsessive disorders and much more.

Carl Jung's Personality Classification Theory

Psychologist Carl Jung classified people on the basis on their sociability quotient into introverts and extroverts. Introverts are folks who are primarily inward driven, shy, withdrawn and reticent. They are more focused on their ideas and sensibilities than the external world around them. Introverts are known to be more logical, reflective and sensible by nature. They take time to crawl out of their box, and establish a rapport with others.

On the other hand, extroverts are outgoing, friendly, affable, social and gregarious people who live more in the present than worry about the future. They have a more positive and exuberant disposition, and are more than willing to accept challenges or changes.

After classifying people as introverts and extroverts, Jung received his share of brickbats from psychologists who believed that the classification was too restrictive to categorize every human being on the planet. Experts argued that a majority of people rarely demonstrated extreme introvert or extrovert tendencies. According to them only a majority of people possess extreme introvert or extrovert tendencies. Most people in fact possess a little bit of both, and their behavior differs according to the situation.

For instance, someone like me enjoys going out and spending time with people but I also value some time alone for reflection and contemplation every now and then. This neither makes me a hardcore extrovert or introvert but more of a combination of both – an ambivert.

Social Learning

This theory talks about how people pick up personality or behavioral traits from their immediate environment. It proposes that an individual's behavior is a result of their growing up conditions and environment. We pick up specific patterns and personality traits through our experiences. Social learning psychologists are of the view that all our behavior is learnt through our social experiences.

For example, if a person has been rewarded in a specific manner, he or she learns behavior through positive reinforcement and experiences. For example, someone throwing excessive tantrums may have learned through their experiences that drama gets them attention. Every time they want attention they know throwing tantrums will do the trick. At times, we don't have to experience something to learn behavior. Our mind is conditioned to use complex codes, information, actions, symbols and consequences. A majority of our observations and vicarious experiences drive our behavior, and help us imbibe specific personality traits.

Ernest Kretschmer's Classification

German psychologist Ernest Kretschmer's personality classification theory theorizes that a person's physical characteristics or personality traits determine the likelihood of a person suffering from mental ailments and their personality.

According to this personality classification, people are classified as Athletic, Pyknic, Dysplastic and Asthenic. Pyknic personality types are people who are round, stout and short. They demonstrate more extrovert traits such as gregariousness, friendliness and an outgoing disposition.

The Aesthetic personality types are people who have a

slender and slim appearance. They have a fundamentally introvert personality. These are folks who have strong, athletic and robust bodies, and demonstrate more aggressive, enthusiastic and energetic characteristics.

Briggs Myers Personality Indicator

There are multiple personality tests that determine an individual's personality type based on a psychological analysis. One of the most widely used personality analysis tests is the Briggs Myers Personality Indicator. It is a comprehensive report that analyzes people's personalities based on how they perceive the world and make decisions.

The Briggs-Myers Personality Indictor was created by Isabel Briggs Myers and Katherine Briggs. It is based on Jung's theory but expounds on it through four primary psychological functions or processes such as sensation, thinking, feeling and intuition.

The MBTI emphasizes on one of the four primary functions dominating over other traits. The personality indicator operates on an assumption that everyone possesses a preference for the manner in which they experience the world around them. These inherent differences emphasize our values, motives, beliefs and interests, and thus determine an overall personality.

There are around 16 distinct personality types based on this psychological personality analysis theory. The Briggs-Myers test comprises several questions, where test respondents reveal their personality through their answers. This test is also widely used in areas such as determining a person's chances of success in a particular role and compatibility in interpersonal relationships.

In Myers Briggs personality theory, a personality type is determined when there is a clear preference for one style over another. Different letters connected with individual preferences helps determine the person's Myers Briggs personality type. For instance, if a person reveals a clear tendency for I, S, T and J, they have the ISTJ personality type.

Extraversion and introversion – The first letter of the Briggs-Myers personality type is related to the direction of one's energy. If a person is externally focused or focused on the external world, they show a preference for extraversion. On the contrary, if the energy is inward directed, the person shows a clear inclination for introversion.

Sensing and Intuition – The second letter is concerned with processing information. If an individual prefers dealing with information, has clarity, can describe what they see etc. then they show a distinct preference for sensing. Intuition, on the other hand, is related to intangible ideas and concepts. Intuition is represented by the letter "N."

Thinking and Feeling – The third letter reflects an individual's decision making personality. People who show an inclination for analytic, logical and detached thinking reveal a tendency for thinking over feeling. Similarly, people who show a preference for feeling are more driven by their values or what they believe in.

CHAPTER 3

BODY LANGUAGES

While information regarding what characteristics a person desires people to see can be readily ascertained from that person's general appearance, information regarding what a person does not necessarily want to convey can be gleaned from that person's body language. This is because people are generally unaware of their bodily reactions to their environment, and people are even less able to control those reactions.

Body language will indicate the inner emotional state and characteristics of a person, such as frustration, fear, nervousness, joy, and honesty. The list can go on and on. These are aspects of a person that cannot usually be seen from their clothing or hairstyle. When a person's general appearance, voice, and/or body language are indicating different things, you should always go with what the person's body language is saying. This is because, again, people are unable to control their involuntary physical reactions.

While body language can reveal the otherwise unseen emotions of a person, it is important to remember that it could simply be indicative of a temporary mental state (i.e., depression), or some kind of physical issue (i.e., an injured leg or back), and may not be probative of any kind of permanent characteristic.

When analyzing a person's body language, as when analyzing anything else, consistency is key. As such, the more information you have about someone's character, the more useful the information gained from analyzing their body language will be to you. This leads us, once again, to the principle that you will need to identify patterns in someone's body language, as well as in their voice and general appearance, in order to draw accurate conclusions.

Practically speaking, body language can be separated into two general categories, those being "open" body language and "closed" body language.

"Open" body language is characterized by someone who is at ease, who directly faces those to with whom they are speaking and who maintain strong eye contact. A person with open body language will also not place their purse, arms, or anything else, in between themselves and the other person.

"Closed" body language can be illustrated by someone who crosses their legs or arms and faces either away from the person to whom they are speaking or be facing off to one side. A person with closed body language would also make sure something is in front of them, thereby forming a barrier between them and the person to whom they are speaking.

Whether someone is exhibiting open or closed body language could tell you something about whether that person is an introvert or extrovert, how comfortable they are in a particular situation, how interested they are in the conversation, how much they like the person to whom they are speaking, and maybe even something about their cultural background.

Interpretation

Body language is tricky because most body positions, postures, and movements can mean many different things or not mean anything at all, depending on the environment. In order to discern what body language signals are significant and which ones are not, you should learn how several basic emotions are generally expressed through various simultaneous movements. In other words, you should try and discern patterns of movements that typically accompany certain emotional states, rather than dragging yourself through the tedious, and often unreliable, practice of committing to memory hundreds of individual physical actions and what the meaning of those actions might be. Common emotions and the body language that typically accompanies them are discussed below.

EMOTIONS

Thoughtful or Focused

The states of either being thoughtful or focused are usually characterized by a person being noticeably devoid of movement. A person's stillness in this instance reveals concentration on either some unspoken string of thought (if thoughtful), or on what the other person is trying to say (if focused). Occasionally, a person who is focused or thoughtful may perform minor movements repetitively, such as tapping a pencil against a table top or twiddling their thumbs. A person who is thoughtful or focused will display this body language unconsciously, and this body language will be present and consistent for extended lengths of time.

Some of the other body language that is indicative of a person being thoughtful or focused includes:

- Holding the head in the hands

- Consistently staring at something

- Consistently maintaining strong eye-contact

- Furrowed brow

- Arms folded with vacant stare

- Looking up

- Laying the chin on fingers or hand

- General absence of movement

- Tilting the head

- Leaning back in the chair

- Scratching the head

Bored

People generally become bored when they do not want to be wherever it is that they are and they do not want to be doing whatever it is that they are doing. When a person is bored and wants to go somewhere else, the body will show signs that it, too, wants to go somewhere else. The tension between wanting to leave and having to stay causes people discomfort. Therefore, people who are bored will generally engage in some physical activity to distract themselves from that discomfort.

Some of the common movements associated with boredom include:

- Eye rolls

- Leaning backwards and forwards in the chair

- Wandering eyes

- Furtive looks at objects such as a watch

- Heavy sighing

- Staring into the distance

- Yawning

- Shifting their weight

- Foot tapping

- Twiddling thumbs

- Finger tapping

- Uncrossing and crossing arms

- Uncrossing and crossing legs

- Scribbling or doodling

- Playing with small objects such as paper clips, pens, coins, etc.

- Pointing the body away from the speaker

- Side to side head movement

- Preening clothes or fingernails

- Stretching

- Trying to do something else

- Holding the chin in the hand and looking around the room

When people are bored, they engage in some kind of physical activity in an attempt to stay attentive. If a bored person does not engage in these physical activities, they may fall asleep. Because of the necessary presence of physical activity, boredom is among the easiest emotional states to spot and among the most difficult to hide.

Some of the signs of boredom are the same or similar to those of someone who is attentive or thoughtful. The key distinction between the two is the absence or presence of movement. Remember that if a person is staring off into space and is completely still, they may be thinking something over. If that same person is staring off into space while fidgeting with something, odds are that person is bored out of their skull.

Angry

An angry person will express that anger by becoming withdrawn, aggressive, or defensive. Anger in the form of aggression is the easiest to spot, being characterized as it is by a flushed face, puffed out chest, a set jaw, tight lips, and a loud and forceful voice. However, many people try not to express their anger so outwardly, or they at least try to control that expression, and will then tend to become withdrawn or defensive.

Some common signs of the three types of anger include:

- Flushed face

- Sarcastic or feigned laughter

- Irritated movement of the arms

- Crossed legs

- Crossed ankles

- Crossed arms

- Finger pointing

- Firm posture

- Phrase repetition

- Lips that are closed tight

- Quick speech

- Quick body movements

- Fixed facial expression or grimace

- Shaking

- Clenched fists

- Set jaw

- General tension

- Quick, shallow, or short breaths

- Hands placed on hips.

- Invasion of personal space

Frustrated

The two forms of frustration are surrender and confrontation. Confrontational frustration is characterized by the person who is under the impression that they can fix whatever it is that is causing the frustration by approaching the problem directly. The signs of confrontational frustration can therefore mirror those that would otherwise indicate anger. The frustration of surrender happens when that irritated person realizes that they cannot fix whatever it is that is irritating them. Surrender frustration is characterized, not by signs indicating anger, but by signs of passive irritation.

Some common signs of frustration of the confrontational variety are:

- Direct and consistent eye contact

- Repetition of certain phrases

- Invasion of personal space

- Should shrugs

- Finger pointing

- Hand gesturing

Signs exhibiting the onset or frustrational surrender include:

- Over-emphasized movement

- Hands to head

- Scowling

- Sighing

- Quick exhalation

- Hands resting on hips

Signs that the frustration of surrender has been reached include:

- Hands thrown in air

- Shoulder shrugging

- Turning away

- Walking away

- Closing the eyes

- Rolling the eyes

- Head shaking

Although confrontational frustration can easily turn into anger, it is important that you not confuse the two and thereby throw off your analysis. It is also important that you do not mistake boredom for surrender type of frustration. While several bored signals mirror those of surrendering out of frustration, people who are bored are not necessary frustrated, just as those who have surrendered to a situation out of frustration are probably not going to be bored.

Depressed

Clinical depression is an animal all its own. Someone suffering from clinical depression may be entirely unable to function, suffer from eating disorders, find concentrating on anything almost impossible, and may disregard their personal hygiene. Clinical depression requires medical treatment. We will not here be describing clinical depression. What we mean here by "depression" is the average type of day-to-day depression that we all have felt at some point in our lives.

Depression affects almost every one of your body's functions, including your body language and voice. Depressed people move and speak differently.

Someone who is depressed will be lethargic and glum. They will be wholly unenthusiastic and tired. Thus, in addition to analyzing someone's body language when searching for signs of depression, remember to pay attention to that person's voice as well (discussed in detail later), as that is another avenue by which depression is sure to manifest itself.

Specific signs of day-to-day depression include:

- Lack of concentration

- Poor memory

- Intentional and slow movement

- Relaxed posture

- Increased appetite

- Decreased appetite

- Slow and quite speech

- Lack of focus

- Eyes downcast

- Isolation

- Diminished capacity to plan in advance

- Lack of attention to personal hygiene

- Lack of attention to personal appearance

Indecisive

Someone who is trying to make a decision between a couple of different options will ordinarily reveal that hesitancy in their body language. People stuck in this position will go back-and-forth in a very real and literal way.

Some signs of indecision include:

- Tipping the head from one side to the other

- Shifting weight back and forth in a chair

- Hands that open and shut

- Hand movements wherein one hand moves, followed by the other

- Looking at one thing, then another, and back again

- Mouth opening and closing without any words being produced.

Nervous

Being nervous, just like being bored, causes discomfort. And, again like boredom, in order to distract themselves from that discomfort, a nervous individual will move their body. Being nervous creates a lot of energy, and a nervous person will need to find something to do with all that extra energy.

Signs that are typical of nervousness include:

- Body tension

- Eyes moving back and forth

- Curling up of the body

- Rocking

- Side to side shifting of weight

- Uncrossing and crossing arms

- Uncrossing and crossing legs

- Tapping hands

- Tapping fingers

- Tapping feet

- Throat clearing

- Lip biting

- Nervous coughing

- Adjustment of, or fidgeting with, hair, jewelry, hands, pens, coins, clothing, fingernails, or any other small object

- Hand squeezing

- Nervous smiling (frequently and rapidly alternating between smiling and not smiling)

- Nervous talking

- Eyes downcast

- Shaking

- Biting finger nails

- Preening cuticles

- Sudden silence

- Upper body rotation from side to side

- Sweating

As you can see, nervousness comes with a great deal of signs, many of which are shared with other emotional states. However, nervous people will generally exhibit more than just one of the signs listed above. Therefore, when analyzing whether someone is nervous or not, look for two or three of these signs to be sure you are not misreading the situation.

Sexual Interest

There are thousands of signs of sexual interest that a person can give. Generally, any behavior that focuses on or emphasizes a person's sexuality could be a clue as to the level of that person's sexual interest.

A very short list of some of the more basic characteristics of behavior that indicates sexual interest includes:

- Slow blinks

- Stares

- Crossing legs (legs crossed towards you would indicate interest, legs crossed away from you would not)

- Uncrossing legs

- Tossing the hair

- Chest thrusted outward

- Hips thrusted outward

- Strutting

- Walking to emphasize curves

- Primping

- Wetting lips

- Winks

- Strong eye contact

- Over-emphasized smile

- Leaning backwards

- Leaning forwards

- Flirtatious smiling

- Close proximity

- Running fingers through hair

- Revealing clothing

- Self-touching (adjusting cuff links, smoothing the skirt, etc.)

- Touching the other (hand on shoulder, patting the hand, hand on knee, etc.

- Using an over-abundance of fragrance or makeup

- Over-dressing

- Deliberately looking the person over ("elevator eyes")

- Intense listening

- Trying to create intimacy, such as by whispering.

- Trying to get the person alone

- Frequently looking at the person

- Exposing the neck (such as by moving the hair)

Resentful

Resentment is usually the end result of jealousy or anger and will generally manifest itself as a cluster of behaviors, the object of which is to distance a person from the object of their resentment.

Signs associated with resentment include:

- Avoiding a person

- Avoiding looking at the person

- Any indication of anger

- Scowling

- Tensing the body

- Crossing arms

- Crossing legs

- Tightly closed or pursed lips

Defensive

Defensiveness is a response to feeling attacked, and will result in the person feeling vulnerable and somewhat awkward. As such, their body language will indicate a desire to circumvent the situation, either verbally or physically.

Many of the indications of a defensive person also apply to a person who is nervous, angry or secretive. Like everything else, the other clues you pick up will point you towards which emotion it actually is.

A defensive person may manifest mannerisms such as:

- Clenched teeth

- Clenched jaw

- Clenched or pursed lips

- Avoiding eye contact

- Body squarely facing person (sign of confrontation)

- Hands resting on hips

- Crossing arms

- Crossing legs

- Crossing ankles

- Abandoning the situation

- Refusal to speak

- Exhaling rapidly

Substance Abuse

Determining whether someone is abusing substances can be extraordinarily difficult because people will try and convince themselves that they are not seeing the signs indicating same, especially if the scrutinized individual is emotionally close to the observer. This is why it is important to stay objective.

Signs of substance abuse include:

- Baggy eyes

- Blood-shot eyes

- Eyes that are only partially open

- Exaggerated behavior (talking too loud, standing too close)

- Very fast speech

- Slurring words

- Rapid and sudden changes in mood

- Shaking

- Flushed face

- Smell

- Lack of personal hygiene

- Isolation

- Skinny legs with an oversized torso (indicative of alcoholism)

- Skinny person with a potbelly (indicative of alcoholism

- Lack of inhibitions

- Considerable inconsistency in behavior from one time to another

- Considerable inconsistency in general appearance from one time to another

How To Use Body Languages To Persuade

The Eyes

Firstly, the eyes. Our eyes operate greatly on their own accord- blinking when they need to and gazing where there is movement. While we can most often control where they look, they will sometimes operate on their own in interactions with others. The eyes will often be the first place to show how the person is feeling.

Our brain and our spinal cord make up the pairing that is known as the central nervous system. This pathway of neurons operates fully automatically- that is to say, with no help from our conscious mind.

The eyes are connected to this nervous system and are the only part of the central nervous system that actually faces the outside of the body. Because of this, the eyes are literally intertwined with what we are thinking and feeling, even more than we notice. The brain and the spinal cord give us life- they are responsible for initiating our movements, our thoughts, and our feelings. "The eyes are the window to the soul" got its origins in this fact of anatomy. That being said, it is very difficult to control the emotions and sentiments that people can see in our eyes as they come directly from the places within us over which we have no control. The eyes, therefore, are the first place to look when it comes to seeing someone's truth.

Eye contact is a big indicator of the intentions of a person. As previously discussed, the amount of eye contact someone is making is an indicator of their level of comfort. If someone is making and holding eye contact for a long period of time without looking away, they appear to be very comfortable to the point of seeming like they may have predetermined intentions.

If someone is avoiding eye contact altogether, they tend to seem very untrustworthy, almost as if they are trying very hard to hide something from you. We have all encountered an uncomfortable amount of eye contact, whether too much or too little, where it made us feel like something was not right. You may have been feeling unease but were unaware as to why.

Feeling someone's eyes staring directly into yours with no end in sight makes for a lot of discomfort while trying to catch someone's eye who is clearly making an effort to avoid yours makes for a very awkward conversation. If someone is making steady eye contact, looking away every now and then and then coming back to meet your eyes once again, they are probably feeling comfortable in the situation or conversation and are quite secure with themselves and their position. This amount of eye contact makes us feel comfortable in the other person's presence and feel that their intentions are pure.

Eye movement is also a type of communication that goes on. The eyes tend to go where the person wants to go. If someone glances at something, chances are they are thinking about it or wishing to go there. For example, if someone glances at a chair in the room, they are probably tired of standing.

If someone glances at the door, they would probably like to leave or may be late for something. If you see someone looking over at another table for the duration of your dinner date, chances are they are wishing they were with someone else.

Think of yourself in this type of situation.

On a date where you feel bored and unenthused, you would probably be searching wildly around the room for an excuse to leave or another person to daydream about. If your date is unaware of what your eye movements are demonstrating, they may keep droning on about the stock market for another hour or two.

While everyone blinks at slightly different rates, you can start to pick up on changes in blinking speed. Watch your partner next time they are sitting across from you and notice how often they blink. Picking up on this will alert you when there is a change in blinking speed. Blinking very often and quickly is said to be an indicator of thinking hard or of stress. What causes your partner to begin blinking quickly? This observation will give you some insight into what causes them stress and mental strain.

Facial Expressions

Subtle movements of the face can be picked up when examining another person closely. These subtle movements are said to happen instinctively when a person has a feeling of intense emotion. They are very difficult to fake as they happen quickly and subtly. These subtle movements can be very telling if we can learn to pick up on them.

The first involuntary facial movement is that of surprise. When genuinely surprised, a human face will drop the jaw, raise the eyebrows and widen the eyes. The second is fear. Fear causes the eyebrows to rise slightly, the upper eyelid to raise and the lips to tense.

The next is disgust, which causes the upper lip to rise and the nose to wrinkle. Anger causes the eyebrows to lower, the lips to come together and the bottom jaw to come forward. Happiness causes the corners of the lips to rise, the cheeks to rise and the outsides of the eyes to wrinkle. This wrinkling of the eyes is indicative of a real smile, as in a fake smile this does not happen.

Sadness involves the outside of the lips to lower, the inside of the eyebrows to raise and the lower lip to come forward. Finally, an intense feeling of hate causes one side of the mouth to raise. These expressions all take place so quickly that they are often missed. If you know what to look for though, you will notice them before they are gone. This will be one of the most accurate ways to analyze a person as they will likely have no idea that this has occurred on their face.

The face has a lot to say when it comes to body language, and with so many small muscles there are a lot of movements that occur unbeknownst to the person being observed. This is a great place to start when it comes to learning to analyze people.

Reading the language of the rest of the body can be better understood when done from the perspective of looking at an animal. Animals' main priority is always to protect themselves if a fight were to occur. They always have their vital areas covered when they are in a vulnerable position or situation and will open up when they feel safe.

Humans are similar in this way. Our vital areas are all in the middle of our body- around our heart and lungs. When we see an animal in a strange setting or around other animals that it may have to fight with it will be positioned in a way where nothing will be able to access its heart, its lungs or its stomach area. Thinking of humans in this way will be a great tool for analyzing them.

Use Powe Poses

Gestures and Facial Expression

You can read so much about someone by looking at their faces. From excitement, surprise, anger, happiness, confusion to sadness, all this is possible when you look at their face. Many people are conflicted because they try to protect another person's feelings. This is why they might say they are happy, but their face says something else.

From the facial expression, you can determine whether you can trust someone or not. In a split second, you can choose whether to trust them or not. If someone is assuring you with a sly grin on their face, it is wise to back off. Confidence and friendliness are often expressed with a light smile and slightly raised eyebrows.

Some people can read your face and tell whether you are intelligent or confident about what you are talking about. A simple question might throw you off your thought pattern and help them get a better perspective of you.

Gestures are direct. The signs associated with gestures

are obvious because some are universal. You can convey different messages from your gestures. They are part of body language that helps you put forward your message without saying something.

In terms of posture, it is always advisable to be assertive. An assertive posture is about confidence. Stand up straight, keep your shoulder and legs aligned, and make sure your weight is evenly distributed on your legs. An assertive posture is about confidence. It shows the person you are communicating with that you are sure of what you are talking about.

There is so much information displayed on your face. Awareness of this might shock you. Whenever you speak to someone, they will listen to your words but, at the same time, try to read your face because of the innocence and genuineness in it. You can mince your words or train as much as you can to present your case in a certain way, but your face will always tell a different story if you are lying.

Besides, by looking at your face, it is easier for someone to feel your emotions, especially if they are keen. While some people have mastered the art and can do it, not everyone can conceal their emotions. All this can be read from your face—your happiness, sadness, dismay, disappointment, elation, and so forth. A keen audience can tell your emotions, regardless of what you say.

Instinctive Cues

Trust your gut. You have heard this so many times. Does it work? It does. In fact, in most cases, you are wrong when you go against your gut. If you have a bad feeling about someone the very moment you meet them, there is a good chance you should trust that feeling and walk away.

Intuition and gut feelings can be accurate and help you get out of a dangerous situation. If you are meeting someone for the first time, you don't know anything about them, and neither do they about you. In your first chance meeting, it is always safe to trust in your gut.

The good thing about trusting your gut is that you don't have to read much into anything. All you need is to be relaxed, listen to what they have to say, and reflect on it. If it doesn't feel right to you, don't force it. Your gut feelings should alert you to monitor other observable cues about someone and use that as a credible way of determining whether they are lying or not.

Personal Vibes

Is it possible to feel a good or bad vibe from someone? It is true. Other than the visual and auditory communication, we can also communicate with people around us by giving off vibes. Vibes are about emotional signaling. The fact that we are social creatures means that naturally we are drawn to socializing and will often feel what someone is feeling by sharing in their vibe even if we are not physically feeling it too.

Take the example of talking to someone who says something that disgusts you. You will feel depressed and might lower your eyebrows or shrink in your seat. If they are keen, this will rub off on them too. Immediately, they realize that something is not right. This is how emotional signaling works. It is a good thing, too, because it allows you to understand each other and communicate faster without having to put up with different constraints in your environment.

In analyzing people, it is wise that you become aware of your environment, and the vibes people give off around you. This way, the vibes, and your gut feeling can always alert you when something is not right. The good thing is that some people are so evil, they give off a negative vibe around them that you cannot miss. Such are the people you need to stay away from.

Once you pick up on the vibe, you can easily trace the communication to other observable features like how their eyes are moving, the tone they use when talking to you, and so forth.

Your Hands

Have you ever watched a politician and how they use their arms and hands? The hand is often swept down in a cutting motion when they want to emphasize what they are saying and comes down emphatically to make each point.

Or have you watched how a comedian will open his arms to his audience with palms up, inviting his audience to share his incredulity at a ridiculous but hilarious occurrence he is describing? Creative people often wave their arms around, especially when they are getting excited about their current topic.

Research has found that babies who use lots of hand gestures at 18 months go on to be more intelligent in later life. We can say all kinds of things with our hands without ever opening our mouths, so we should get on and incorporate them into our lives as soon as possible.

Using our hands and arms comes naturally. Even blind people do it when speaking to other blind people. However, be aware that there are limits. You should not be waving your arms around like a windmill because that just becomes distracting and people cannot concentrate on what you're saying. So, let's get down to business and find out what we should be doing.

HANDS

Counting

Children learn to count using their fingers – and sometimes their toes – but it is often used in normal speech to emphasize what you are saying and helps others to remember. So, for instance, if you order three coffees in a busy café, and hold up three fingers at the same time, the server has a visual record as well as an audio one of how many you ordered.

Just a Tiny Bit

Holding your forefinger and thumb slightly apart indicates that you mean 'just a little'. You might do this to emphasize that you only want a very small amount if someone asks you if you want pepper on your food for instance.

Nothing to Hide

Holding both palms up indicates that you have nothing to hide and you are revealing that there is nothing in your hands. It is also an invitation for someone else or an audience to share something you are saying. This gesture could also be used to ask for compassion from someone else.

Stop Right There!

One palm up, pointing towards the other person(s), might be used to stop someone in their tracks when they are speaking. It might mean that you think that the person is under a misapprehension and it is an indication that you want to take back control in the conversation. It is the same gesture as a traffic cop might use to stop the traffic.

And, what's more......

This is a pointed finger in the direction of the person you are speaking to. But take care with this one because if it's done sharply and with a prodding motion, it can quite easily be perceived to be aggressive.

Whatever

Holding up your hands so that your palms face each other and loosely shaking them indicates that something can be one thing or another. It can represent flexibility and that there is nothing firmly fixed in place.

Making a Distinction

This is when you might raise one hand loosely to represent one point of view and the other hand then comes us as you home in on the other point of view. It's about delineating two points of view.

From Here to Here

Holding your hands facing each other and then moving them in or out can indicate growth or shrinkage.

Growth

Holding one palm facing downwards and then raising it indicates growth or shrinkage if used the other way of course.

And that includes you

This brings someone back to the conversation if you mind detect that their mind is wandering. It might mean, 'And I'm sure that you feel the same?' It gives grounds of commonality so that the person feels more attuned to what you are saying.

And I'm talking from the heart here

Holding both hands towards the chest or the heart means that what you are saying is heartfelt and that it is personally how you feel.

Let's go for it

Making a fist shows that you are about to make a determined effort. Watch the facial expressions when making a fist though because it can also mean that you're edging for a fight.

Let's put all that aside for now

Making a sweeping movement with your hands can indicate that you want to ignore what's gone before and lay out fresh information. Or it could mean that you want to amalgamate all the facts available.

Let's get cracking

This means that someone is eager to get started with something and shows enthusiasm. Alternatively, it could mean an anticipation of gain.

Now I feel confident

The gesture of clasping your own hands over your abdomen or crotch should be used if you want to feel more secure. It's used as a symbolic sign of protection. Watch out for others doing this because the higher that the hands are held, the higher the level of insecurity.

I'm the boss

When hands are clasped behind the back it normally indicates authority. Members of the English royal family often adopt this stance, but it could equally be used by an army sergeant or university lecturer. It shouts out that that person is confident because they are brave enough to expose their front body without feeling the need of protection.

ARMS

I'm trying to restrain myself

When someone is holding on to their arm behind their back, they are holding themselves back. They may find themselves becoming irritated and this is a way of keeping themselves in check against attack be that physical or verbal. It's done behind the back because the person doing it doesn't want to appear negative or aggressive to the other person.

United we Stand

Holding your arms out and then joining them together means that you are encompassing the other person(s) into what you are saying so that it unites you. Your fingers might intertwine to show extra solidarity. If you do this whilst facing someone, you might encircle your arms around them to say that they are part of your inner circle and that you trust them.

I am so bored

We are probably all very familiar with this one and it is represented quite clearly by crossed arms in front of the body. The body assumes a relaxed position because it feels disinterested and is switching off. It can also indicate a level of defensiveness, ostensibly protecting the main organs of the body. Watch out if the person's fists are clenched at the same time though because it can mean aggressiveness.

I'm safe

One arm across the chest with the hand clasping the other arm emulates when we were children and our parents hugged us. It provides us with comfort and reassurance.

I'm Waiting

Standing with your arms out with one hand on either side of your waist would indicate that someone is waiting with a reducing level of patience. Alternatively, it might also mean that someone is ready for the next step.

Of course, there are many more gestures, but this list

provides some of the most common and those that you should bear particular attention to. If you want to keep your thoughts to yourself, you better be sure to sit on your hands at the same time.

In the Western world, when we greet someone formally or perhaps for the first time, it is usual to use the handshake. This can be just as intimate as the French embrace because you are putting your palm into someone else's bare palm and may even pull them into your own personal space. The handshake evolved as a sign of greeting and whilst on the Orient they used a simple bow, in the West the handshake was used, palm meeting palm, to show that they were carrying no weapon and no evil intent. In ancient Rome, the greeting was made by clasping someone higher up on the forearm because they frequently carried daggers hidden near their wrists up their sleeves.

You might be meeting someone for the first time or using it as a greeting an associate or friend. Either way, it should be a firm grip and not last too long. When you shake the person' hand, look them in the eyes and have a slight friendly smile.

It all sounds rather straightforward but even a simple handshake can be adapted to take on many meanings. Some of those meanings have been allocated almost universally so that the initiator of the handshake will adopt a certain type of handshake to impress that assumption on the other person. In other cases, the assumption made about the other person is not necessarily complimentary but may indicate a weak personality, for instance.

There are many types of handshake, even though the action might sound quite straightforward and perfunctory. Outlined are the most common below.

Firm Handshake

This is as described above and would be preferable for new introductions or, indeed, for most situations. It shows no assumption of dominance or control but is about people meeting or greeting on equal terms.

Sweaty Palms

This might indicate a feeling of nervousness. If you're interviewing someone and their palm is damp, take this into consideration. If you come up a salesman with a sweaty palm, he is either desperate for the commission or he might not have that much faith in his product. Be sure to check it out thoroughly before committing. However, you should also be aware the 5% of the population suffer from excessive sweating that they cannot control and which is not a sign of nervousness.

Politician's Handshake

This is when the other person cover's your hand with their other hand so that it is encased between both of theirs. The hand grasping yours is firm. This handshake can be used between friends when it is indicates closeness between the two of you. This might even escalate into a sandwich of four hands if you are especially close or if someone is trying to achieve the illusion of it. Or it might involve the other person grasping your upper arm with their other hand, but this is normally only when a close bond exists between the two people involved.

However, when someone who does not know you very well adopts it, they are trying to emulate that closeness which is normally insincere. Don't be too ready to put your trust in them. A handshake is devised to keep someone in their place and keep a distance between two bodies.

Dead Fish

This is a limp shake and is normally given by someone you might regard as being wishy-washy, a bit of an insubstantial personality with nothing to bring to the table. This type of person is unlikely to be a people person.

Bone Crusher

This is used by someone who wants to assert their dominance in the relationship. They might use it to test the strength of the other person. However, it should be avoided as people who use this type of handshake are normally regarded as bombastic and overbearing.

Lobster Claw

This is when the other person's palm does not touch yours, but they put their fingertips to your palm instead. This shows a level of unwillingness to commit to being open with you and this type of person may have problems building meaningful relationships. They refuse to show too much of themselves and share information. Give them time to build their trust in you and don't try to rush them.

Finger Vice

This is when the other person grips your fingers instead of meeting palm to palm. It is an indication of assumed dominance and they want to keep you in your place and control you. They want to show their superiority over you most likely out of insecurity. Don't show any weakness but if it helps you get what you want you should treat them with respect.

Tea Cup

This is like a normal handshake, but the palms do not touch. It can indicate that the person is hiding something from you or not giving you all the information you should have to make a reasoned decision. If you are doing business with this person, check the facts before signing on the dotted line.

Dominator

This is when the person shakes your hand using a normal grip, but their palm is on top, facing the floor. This would indicate a show of dominance because your hand is on the bottom being forced into submission. If you want to let the other person they are in charge, adopt the stance of submission and the other person will feel a false sense of security in their power.

Queen's Fingertips

This is one that might be used between a woman and a man when the woman offers her hand face down as if she were expecting it to be kissed. It is normally a sign that the person prefers to keep more personal space between themselves and the other person, so she doesn't want the intimacy of a full handshake. It forces the other person to shake the fingers of the person offering their hand in this fashion and may indicate that the person doing so regards themselves as superior.

As can be seen from above, there are many types of handshake and the same person might use different types in different situations. None of them will give you a totally foolproof reading of another person but they are often a good indication of what you might expect as your relationship proceeds.

A handshake might also be used to say goodbye or seal a deal. Notice if the handshake is the same as the one the other person used to greet you. It may be that you've won them round and that initial handshake gave you the information about how to play it and get them to sign the contract.

Your Mouth

The Mouth

Another place to look on the face is the mouth. The mouth's subtle movements often go completely unnoticed by the person themselves. We will examine a smile for instance.

A genuine smile will include a change or movement in all parts of the face, this happens automatically and is not controlled by the person. A fake smile, however, will only involve the movement of the mouth into the desired shape of a smile and not involve the eyes or the upper areas of the face. These two types of smiles can tell a great deal about what a person is thinking.

A real and genuine smile indicates that the person is happy and interested, while a fake smile indicates that the person wants approval or acceptance. Another type of smile is one that includes the movement of only one side of the mouth. This type indicates that the person is feeling unsure or not convinced.

CHAPTER 4

EFFECTIVELY ANALYZING PEOPLE THROUGH THEIR WORDS

Everything that a person does or says reveals something about their personality. Actions, beliefs, and thoughts of people are aligned perfectly with each other in a way that they all reveal the same things concerning an individual. Just as it is said that all methods can lead to Rome, everything a person thinks or does can reveal a lot about their personality makeup and personality. The words that are spoken by a person, even if they appear to carry less weight, tell a great deal about a person's insecurities and desires.

No one doubts that the words we speak or write are a full expression of our inner personalities and thoughts. However, beyond the real content of a language, exclusive insights into the minds of the author are usually hidden in the text's style.

From our acts of dominance to truthfulness, we are revealing to others too much about us. You can quickly know the most important of all the people in the room by listening to the words that they use. Confident and high-status people use very few "I" words. The higher a person's status is in a given situation, the less the "I" words they will use in their conversations.

Each time people feel confident, they tend to focus on the task that they have at hand, and not necessarily on them. "I" is also used less in the weeks that follow a given cultural upheaval. As age kicks on, we tend to use more positive emotional words and even make very fewer references to ourselves. A study has also shown it that the higher social class a person is, the fewer emotional words he will need to use.

According to Pennebaker, style words include auxiliary verbs, prepositions, pronouns, articles, and conjunctions. He also goes ahead to explain the content words, which include regular verbs, nouns, and especially adverbs and adjectives. Here is the main difference between the style words and the content words. The content words are what someone is saying while the style words are how the words are said.

Women tend to use pronouns, social words, negations,

as well as references to the psychological processes as compared to the male. This could be a surprise, but men tend to use more big numbers, prepositions, and articles than women. But despite all that, the way women speak implies that human beings are more open and self-aware to the self-reflection. That is, according to Pennebaker, who also discovered that there are three main ways in which people speak when they are not saying the truth. He also discovered that the health of a person is likely to improve, not with the increased application of the emotion words such as joyful, happy, and sad, but with more use of the cognitive words such as understand, realize and know. Public figures who have the tendency of addressing press briefings tend to use more first-person singular each time they are prone to committing suicide or troubled. When people tell the truth, they are likely to use the pronouns of the first person singular more often than other times. When the levels of testosterone increase in people, they will tend to drop in their use of references to other people that they are talking to.

Another study has also shown it that people who talk about traumatic circumstances or decodes to share some moments of feeling down or painful truth are physically healthier as opposed to those who kept the experiences secret.

I earned another honorary degree.

The word clue in this sentence is "another." It is used to give a notion that the speaker has earned more than one previous honorary degrees. The person wanted to prove to others that he/she has earned at least one honorary degree. It is a smart way of bolstering the self-image of a person. The speaker may require the admiration of others to be able to show his/her self-esteem. Professional observers could exploit this kind of vulnerability by using flattery and comments that can help in enhancing the ego of the speaker.

I have worked so hard to achieve my goal.

The word clue in this sentence is "hard." It suggests that the speaker values goals that appear so hard to achieve. The sentence might also indicate that the goals that the person has made could be more difficult to achieve than the goals that he usually attempts to achieve. The word clue in this sentence also offers other suggestions. It also shows that the speaker can defer gratification or strongly believes that dedication and hard work tend to produce a better result. A job seeker that has the following characteristics stands higher chances of getting a job because the character traits could be attractive to the employers. It is because this is a kind of individual who would accept challenges and have the determination to be able to finish up tasks in a successful way.

I patiently sat through the public lecture forum.

The word clue in this sentence is "patiently'. It can be used in many hypotheses. It could mean that the person could have been bored with the public lecture forum. Perhaps the person was forced to talk on the phone or even use the restroom. No matter the kind of reason, the person has evidently preoccupied with other things apart from the main contents of the public lecture forum. Someone who patiently waits for a break before leaving a forum or a room is someone who obeys the social etiquette and norms.

A person whose phone rings and gets up immediately and leaves the room shows that they do not have strong rigid for the social boundaries. Those who have social barriers stand higher chances of getting job opportunities because they not only respect the authorities but also follow the rules to the later. Employers will analyze the characters of these people by listening to the kind of speeches that they offer.

On the other hand, someone who fails to follow the social conventions would stand a chance of getting a job that needs novel thinking. Someone who has the predisposition to act outside the social norms would make a good spy as opposed to someone who is disposed to follow the social conventions. This is because spies are usually asked to violate the social norms on a routine.

I opted to purchase that model.

The word clue in this sentence is "opted." It shows that the person weighs a few options before deciding to make the final purchase. At times, they could have struggled to some extent before making the final decision to buy what they wanted. The behavior trait showcased here is that this is a person who thinks through making the decision to buy something. The word "opted" can also be used to show that this person is not likely to be impulsive. Someone impulsive would likely use words such as "I just purchased that model'. The word clue in this second sentence is "just" and suggests that the person just purchased the item without giving it much though.

Based on the first-word clue of "opted," the listener can go ahead and develop a hypothesis that the speaker is an introvert. Introverts are the type of people who usually think before they decide. However, they tend to carefully weigh on each of the options that they have before giving their views and decision. Introverts, on the other hand, tend to be more impulsive. The use of the verb "opted" does not identify the speaker as an introvert in a positive manner, but it seeks to offer an indication that the person could be an introvert.

A detailed personality test needs a more definitive psychological assessment. However, an observer is still able to exploit a person if he is aware that the person tends towards the side of introversion and extroversion.

Extroverts are the kind of people who would get their energy from spending time with other people and look for stimulation from their surroundings. They also tend to speak spontaneously without having a second thought and use the trial and error methods more confidently. The introverts, on the other hand, tend to expend the energy that they got when they socially engage and seek some lonely time to perform other errands.

Introverts will usually look for stimulation from within and rarely speak without having a second thought. They carefully weigh the options that they have before making any decision. Before entering into any kind of business negotiations, knowing whether your opponent tends either towards introversion or extroversion can give a very strategic benefit. Salespeople should give their introverted customers to think about the sales proposals that they are presented to them.

The introverts tend to mull in the information that they got before they can come to a final decision. When the introverts are pressed to make impulsive decisions, they might be forced to say "No," even when they meant "Yes." This is because these people are not comfortable when it comes to making any immediate decision. Conversely, the extroverts can be pressed to certain levels to make quick decisions since they are more at ease when it comes to making impulsive decisions. In very rare cases do people show fully introverted features or entirely extroverted features.

The personality traits of a person tend to slide along a given continuum. There are also several people who show both the introverted and extroverted characters at the same time. In addition to that, those who are introverts appear to be comfortable with their environments and will usually showcase behaviors that are related to the extroversion behaviors. Extroverts can also display the introverted features at times.

What I did was the right thing.

The words clue in this sentence is "right." It is used to suggest that the speaker struggled with an ethical, moral, and legal dilemma and managed to overcome some degree of external and internal opposition to make a just and fair decision. According to the behavioral trait that is portrayed in this sentence, it is also very evident that the person has enough strength of character to be able to make the best and right decision even when pressed with several opposing views. The key here is to listen to what they are saying and let their words do the talking.

Open Communication

In most interpersonal interactions, the first few seconds are very vital. Your first impressions have a great impact on the success of future and further verbal communication with another person. When you first meet a person, you create an immediate impression of them; this is based on how they behave, sound, and look, as well as anything else you may have heard about them.

For example, when you meet a person and hear them speak, you create a judgment about their level of understanding and ability and their background. When you hear a foreign accent, for example, you might decide that you require to use simpler language for communication. You might realize that you need to listen more attentively to make sure that you understand what the person is saying.

Effective Verbal Communication

Effective speaking includes three main stages, that is, words that you choose to use, how you utter the words, and how you reinforce the words. All these areas have an impact on the transmission of your message and how the message is received and understood by the target audience.

It will be important for you to wisely and carefully choose the words to use. You will need to use different words in different events; even you are discussing a similar topic.

How you speak will include your pace and tone of voice. The pace and tone of voice communicate a certain message to the audience, for example, about your level of commitment and interest, or whether you are nervous about the audience reaction.

Active Listening

Effective listening is important for effective verbal communication. Ways that you can ensure that you listen more. These include:

- Be prepared to listen. Focus on the person speaking and not how you are going to reply to them

- Keeping an open mind while you avoid being judgmental about the person speaking.

- Always be objective

- Always focus on the objectivity of the message being conveyed

- Avoid distractions.

- Don't stereotype the person who's speaking.

Enhancing Verbal Communication

Techniques and tools that you can make use of to enhance the effectiveness of your verbal communication. These include:

- Clarifying and Reflecting. It is a process involving giving feedback to another person of your understanding of what has been conveyed or said.

Reflecting usually involves paraphrasing the message that has been conveyed to you by the speaker in your own words. All that you need to do is to capture the importance of the feelings and facts expressed, and communicate your understanding back to the speaker.

Reflecting is an important skill because:

- You are demonstrating that you consider the other person's opinions

- The speaker received feedback about how the message has been received

- Shows respect for, and interest in, what the other person has to say

- You can view what you might have understood the message properly

- *Questioning*. This is how broad we get more information from others on particular topics. It's an important way of clarifying aspects that are not clear or test your understanding. Questioning enables you to seek support from other people explicitly.

Questioning is a vital technique because it helps you to draw another person into a conversation or simply to show interest.

Types of Questions

Open question. These types of questions demand further elaboration and discussion. They help to broaden the scope of reply or response. These types of questions often take long to reply but give the other person a broader scope for encouraging and self-expression involvement in the interaction.

Closed question. They seek only two or one-word answer, often simply 'no' or 'yes.' They allow the person asking the questions to be in total control of the interaction.

CHAPTER 6

PERSONALITY AND BIRTH ORDER

Nope, the effect of birth order on personality type is not just pop psychology, BuzzFeed quiz-style talk. It is in fact based on consistent research and scientific principles. Chuck aside the entertainment and stereotypes, and you have a near accurate technique for determining someone's personality. There are plenty of psychological principles behind the amusing stereotypes that determine people's personalities depending on their birth order.

Why Does Birth Order Impact Our Personality?

According to some psychologists, birth order is as crucial as genetics in determining an individual's personality. It boils down to the nature versus nurture personality debate. Research has pointed to the fact that birth order can indeed influence our personality owing to the fact that the way parents relate to every child of theirs (based on his or her order of birth) is different. Children from the same household never assume the same role.

There is always a clear demarcation of roles and equations between the parents and children vary based on their birth order. For instance, if you are the oldest among siblings and assume the role of a caretaking sibling, no one else will fill that role. The others will then pick other roles, says an achiever or provider.

Parents are almost always directed by a different approach at the birth and subsequent upbringing of each child. The firstborn instills a sense of pride and paranoia in parents. If you are a parent, you'll understand how frightened you were at each potential injury of your firstborn. Similarly, the middle born is often bossed over or dominated by the firstborn sibling, who is already sufficiently acquainted with the ways of the world. The older sibling is viewed as wiser, responsible, and competent.

Compared to the firstborn, the other children are less likely to be micro-managed by the parents, thus changing the equation between them slightly. Parents are more exhausted and worn out by the time the later siblings arrive.

They most likely realize that their fears are unfounded

and that the baby doesn't really need to be micromanaged. Thus, parents turn slightly more flexible when it comes to disciplining and attending to later children. Therefore, middle and younger siblings learn to attract attention.

It isn't a biological process where just because you jumped out of your mother's tummy first, you are destined to be a leader. Rather, it is about how the parents treated the child depending on this birth order that leads to the child developing a specific personality.

Since the firstborn is more of an experiment for the parents, there is a greater tendency to be overly obsessed with minute details, thus leading the child to be a perfectionist. On the other hand, the youngest born child is born when the parents have already figured things out.

The youngest child is also competing for attention with older siblings, which makes him more of a people please and less obsessed with the idea of perfection.

The First Born

The firstborn child in a household is often believed to

be ambitious, dominating, and responsible. They are known to be natural leaders and often lead by example. These are the folks people often look up to for guidance and solutions. They operate with a deep sense of responsibility and are goal-driven.

Since firstborn children enjoy undivided attention, at least for some time from their parents, they are naturally used to being in the front or limelight. They feel like there's no competition and that they are born to lead. It can be seen as a byproduct of the attention showered on them in the absence of other siblings.

The firstborn child may connect more effectively with other firstborns than his or her siblings owing to the birth order. Parents often rely on their firstborns to assist with taking care of their younger siblings, which makes them responsible and reliable.

They are more often than not well-behaved, meticulous, caring, and conscientious. This comes from the idea that others rely on them. From childhood, they've been conditioned to believe that others are dependent on them for support and guidance.

It isn't surprising then that they turn out to be high achievers who constantly seek validation and appreciation from others. They also tend to have a dominating personality and are perfectionists by nature. The older siblings assume the role of a mini parent while also being insecure at the prospect of losing the parents' undivided attention.

The Middle Born

The general notion about middle born children is that they have a high sense of fairness and peace.

Middle children are generally understanding, adjusting, co-operative, yet competitive. They are likely to have a close set of friends, who give them the attention they've not got from the family. Middle children often receive the least attention and affection from the parents, which makes them turn outside the house for forging more meaningful relationships.

They are generally late bloomers and find their calling after much deliberation and experimentation. However, middle born people are often at the helm of powerful and authoritative careers that let them use their slick negotiation skills. This helps compensate for all the attention they probably didn't get as children.

The personality traits of a middle child are

diagrammatically opposite to the characteristics of the first and young child. However, they are unique, juxtaposed between siblings and this role makes them expert negotiators. They quickly learn to navigate their way through tricky and awkward situations. This equips them for entrepreneurship and other positions of authority.

Youngest Child

By the time the youngest child is born, the parents are fairly assured of their expertise as caregivers. They are no longer paranoid or hesitation about their skills as parents. This makes them more flexible and lenient towards the youngest child. There isn't a tendency to monitor every move of the child, which makes more independent. Younger siblings generally enjoy more freedom and thus become independent thinkers and decision-makers. The youngest and oldest children have few traits in common because they've both been brought up with a high sense of self-entitlement.

They've both been made to feel special based on their oldest and youngest positions in the household. Younger siblings have always learned to deal with their parents' divided attention. They are fairly adept at handling competition and aren't bogged by feelings of insecurity and jealousy. They operate with a sense of security and often know their place.

Since the parents are more flexible with them, youngest born people often tend to follow their hearts calling. You will find them in more creatively stimulating professions such as stand-up comedians, actors, painters, writers, and dancers.

The youngest born tends to take more risks, have an untamed spirit, and are often exceedingly charming. If someone tells you they are the youngest sibling in the family, they almost always know how to wriggle out any situation by using their charm. Don't forget to overlook the context though when you're analyzing people.

Sweeping judgments don't work very well when it comes to analyzing people. There may be several things to consider such as situation, setting, context, and culture. In your over-enthusiasm to read people, you may end up making incorrect observations by overlooking context.

The Lone Rangers

Yes, I know what you are wondering. What if you happen to be the only child and don't fit into any order of birth? Lone rangers or the "only child" is often more mature and confident. They tend to think beyond their years owing to the fact the lone rangers are almost always surrounded only by adults in the household. In the absence of siblings, much of their interaction is only with grown-ups of the household.

Having spent a lot of alone time, they become more confident, independent, solution-oriented, creative, and resourceful. Lone rangers have a lot in common with firstborn children. They also share the self-entitlement and feeling of specialness that is associated with the youngest siblings.

Is It Always True?

It may not always be true because parents are known to set extremely high expectations for the firstborn. When first born children do not meet their parent's expectations, they can become highly rebellious. There is a rejection of his or her role.

It is true that most middle born children are excellent

peacekeepers and negotiators because they neither have the rights of the oldest sibling nor the special privileges of the youngest sibling. Caught in the middle, they learn to negotiate their way through life and become exceptionally good peacemakers.

They are more emotionally connected to their friends, owing to the fact that they don't receive the desired attention from the family. They tend to become social butterflies who spend more time outside the house.

It is a known fact that parents aren't as stringent or careful about their youngest child since they are fairly experienced in raising children. They have already seen their older children grow with the required trial and error, and are hence more at peace. A majority of the time, parents are more financially independent by the time their youngest child is born. Thus, the overall feeling of contentment, security, and leniency towards them is high.

Sometimes, the youngest children don't fancy being the baby of their household. There is an increased need to be taken more seriously. This drives them to be more serious about their responsibilities.

Always pay close attention to how people refer to their

birth order while speaking about it. Do they appear more positive or negative about their position? This reveals a lot about whether their birth order has been a bane or boon while influencing their personality. Similarly, observe people's body language while they are speaking about their birth order.

Factors Impacting This Structure

Birth order is not a precise science for determining an individual's personality. It is a good practice to try and know more about an individual's siblings if you are trying to read their personality based on birth order. In addition to birth order, there are several other determinants of who a person turns out to be.

The Natural Elements

Genetics is the single most influential determinant of an individual's personality. About 50 percent of who we are is determined by our genetic make-up. A majority of our personality is influenced by natural, in-born factors.

Gender

Other than birth order, gender also influences who we

become or the roles we assume within our household. For instance, if the firstborn is a son, and the second born is a daughter, they will each have their own gender-based identity.

The daughter will not be bogged down by the pressure of living up to the boy's accomplishments and responsibilities. If the second child was a son, he would've probably experienced the pressure of living up to the older man's achievements. However, since it is a girl, the pressures are not as marked since she will have an identity of her own based on her personality.

Communicating With People Based on Their Birth Order

First Born

Firstborns on account of their undivided attention status, at least for some years, tend to be dominating, leading and controlling by nature. There are in fact two categories of firstborns. The first is the rule-abiding, responsible, and the compliant firstborn type who strives to be an example for their siblings.

The second category is aggressive and dominating leaders who know how to get things done owing to their perfectionist ways. Be a good team player, follow the rules, and demonstrate a caring approach towards the former category. Similarly, seek the expertise, and stick to perfect ways of the second type. The leaders enjoy being in control and issuing instructions, so you need to be a good follower while dealing with them. They derive a great sense of importance when people ask for expertise or guidance.

Middle Borns

Middle borns are often known to be rebellious by nature since they do not enjoy the special privileges of the first and last born. They often do not get the attention enjoyed by the firstborn or the special pampering received by the second born.

Showering them with special attention or offering genuine compliments is a great way to get into their good books. They tend to be either outgoing or lonely. Try to win the confidence of the lonely middleborns without pushing them to open up.

Give them their time and space, and you'll do well. Do not rush them into anything. Similarly, if you're negotiating with them, you better be excellent at the game because middleborns can be exceptionally gifted negotiators.

Handle the rebellious with gentle firmness. Be assertive yet polite while communicating them. They are good at compromising in any situation, which is why they also quickly take to peacemakers and solution providers.

Avoid confrontation and deal with them in a more sensitive, and accommodating manner. Learn to be more compromising and adjusting while dealing with them.

They may have issues with assertiveness, confidence, and self-esteem. Keep this mind while interacting with them. Boost their self-esteem while interacting with them, and you'll win brownie points with them.

Last Borns

Last borns on account of being "the baby of the family" generally become less self-reliant and independent compared to their siblings. They can often be unrelenting and stubborn. The best way to deal with them is to shower them with attention and affection. They are happy to take suggestions and advice because they aren't very independent thinkers. Don't try to negotiate with them as when they make up their mind, they are almost always sure.

CHAPTER 7

PERSONALITY TYPES AND PATTERNS

We use the different types of personalities to know the strengths of each person.

Let us look at the different kinds of people that you will come across.

Most people have a general idea of being shy, daring, outgoing, or charismatic. But this is not all when you understand the personality type you get to enjoy many benefits that include:

Knowing Other People's Preferences

Every person has his or her own preferences, and you can judge these by knowing the personality type.

When these people operate within the preferences, you get them to be more effective and efficient. However, operating outside the preferences requires more type and energy.

Knowing if you are within the boundaries can help you

improve efficiency, productivity, and even grow management skills.

Avoid Conflict

Understanding the type of person you depend on the personality type helps you avoid any conflict.

You get to diffuse them way before they come up. If you know that your personality makes you intense whenever a situation arises, you will adjust the behaviour so that you are more receptive to the issue.

When you are usually the one to accept responsibility even when you aren't the one that messed things up, you get o train yourself to become more analytical and take time to evaluate the situation before you handle it.

Helps You Appreciate Diversity

Once you know your personality type, you have the chance to interact with other people and appreciate how diverse they are.

When you are in a work environment, the chances are that at times you will hit a roadblock and end up failing to handle some situations.

When this happens, it is good to have a mind that will take up the issue on your behalf and implement it.

Find the Right Career

The personality type you adopt plays a huge role in the type of job that you are suited to.

It also affects how you handle the job that you are given.

The type of personality you have helps you find the right career that will give you proper job satisfaction. For instance, if you are an extrovert, you will find it hard to work in a position that requires you to work alone.

On the other hand, if you are an introvert, you will find it hard to work in a position that doesn't give you the chance to work alone.

Make Better Decisions

How you make decisions based more on what you see and past experience.

You know that when you take a certain decision, you will either end up with something good or you will lose out.

It also bases on sensing and intuition.

If you decide to make a decision based on sense, then you will engage all your fixe senses to gather information, analyze it then make the right decision.

On the other hand, if you use intuition to make a decision, you will most likely feel the situation before you can make a choice.

The only downside to analyzing issues before you make a decision is that you will tend to analyze the issues longer than necessary, which in turn makes the decision to take longer than expected.

The theory behind having a personality type is that we get born with it, and then we live with it before finally dying with it.

When faced with a situation, we have the chance to apply the personality type the right way spending on the scenario or experiences

> The personality types are based on Myers-Briggs theory that was developed by a partnership between a mother and daughter combination.

> Let us look at the combination pairs that make the theory applicable in all situations:

Extraversion and Introversion

This is concerned with the way you direct your energy.

If your energy is mostly directed towards dealing with people, situations, and things, then you are an Extravert (E).

On the other hand, if you direct your energy towards your inner world, then you are a perfect example of an introvert (I).

Sensing and Intuition

This looks at the kind of information that you end up processing.

If you are one to look at facts, analyze them, and then come up with a decision from the facts, then you are a sensor (S).

On the other hand, if you are one that makes your decisions without having to analyze facts, then you are intuitive (N)

Thinking and Feeling

This looks at your personality type, depending on your decision-making style.

If you base your decisions on the basis of logic, taking time to analyze and come up with the best approach, then you prefer Thinking (T).

If on the other hand, you prefer to use values, which means you make decisions based on what you see is important, then you are in for Feeling (F)

Judgment and Perception

This is the final pair that you can use to determine your personality type.

If you plan your life in a structured way, then you have a preference for Judging (J).

If on the other hand, you have a preference of going along with the flow, responding to things as they come along, then you are in for Perception (P).

Understanding the Scope and Limitations of Personality Analysis

At this point you may be thinking that if learning personality analysis is so advantageous, why doesn't everyone do it?

It may be difficult for the budding psychoanalyst to believe, but the biggest reason is that most people simply aren't interested in learning this skill, much less putting in the effort to master it. People in general are focused on their own lives and how they can affect change in their immediate surroundings.

By being willing to explore this field of knowledge, you are already well on your way to becoming a master of human psychology and personality analysis and will likely gain a huge leg up advantage in any social situation.

It must be mentioned, however, that this is also a skill that requires time and practice of careful observation of others. This isn't a skill that is going to all fall into place overnight, but with consistent observation of human nature, applied over time, you will find yourself becoming extremely perceptive of people's motivations and have a greater capacity to be able to manipulate and influence others to your advantage.

Luckily, we have compiled in this book some fantastic shortcuts to fasttrack you on your progress to becoming a master of human manipulation.

The other aspect of personality analysis to consider here is that you must be gathering data within a framework that allows to to most efficiently analyze and put to use what you are observing. Without a framework to understand your observations, you will be spending much more time trying to gain a foothold on any observations you have made, no matter how carefully or objectively.

By incorporating a framework in your analysis, you will be able to sift out the data that is most relevant to you and know what line of inquiry to take when dissecting someone's personality. After reading this book and applying what you have learned, you will be well versed in the personality analysis systems which will yield great and useful information.

Let's dive a little deeper into the two main aspects of analyzing people: the analysis framework, and cold reading.

The Analysis Framework

The first aspect of personality analysis is building a framework, or creating the foundation that you will need to be able to interpret data gathered from your observations.

When you look at a group of people, for instance, it can be overwhelming to consider the mass of collective experiences, thoughts, emotions, and behaviours that the group represents.

That's why it is so important to have a framework, a lens through which to understand other people's perspectives. The framework that you will develop will consists of a series of reference points for categorizing behaviours.

This framework will allow you to understand someone's personality intimately - so so that you can understand what they do 99% of the time. Knowing their patterns, and why they act the way they do now, you will be able to predict with a degree of accuracy what they are likely to do in the future. The key is understanding the why's behind their behavior.

By sorting people into various categories, you will begin to understand why they act a certain way, and their perspective will become clear to you.

Habits, tendencies, likes, dislikes...Their predominant desires, motivations, fears and consistent thought patterns will all become easy for you to read and interpret.

Another amazing thing about this type of analysis is

that once you are familiar with your target's personality (ie. have spent some amount of time with them observing their behavior) you can even do much of this analysis even away from the subject in question, without them even knowing about it, and without asking them questions that may be considered impertinent or that may give away your own motivations.

Cold Reading

This brings us to the second tool for personality analysis that we will be discussing in this book: cold reading.

Where the analysis framework is more of a scientific process of understanding social dynamics and theory, cold reading is more about the art of careful observation.

Cold reading is being able to understand what is going on in your target's mind at any given moment.

The skills that are relevant to developing cold reading abilities are:

- General body language analysis including

analyzing eye movements, gestures and voice intonation;

- Lie detection, and comparing & matching verbal and non-verbal cues;

- Understanding your own cognitive biases; and

- Developing your own intuition

That may sound complicated, and as if there is a lot of abilities that you need to put a lot of effort into learning. But after you understand the basics of body language and gain a handle on the information, you will find that all it takes is practice, and a little bit of patience, to become very good at cold reading.

Cold reading is essential to analyzing people effectively because it allows you to gather a very large amount of data on the other person, especially if you strive to maintain objectivity in your interactions.

Someone who is very good at cold reading will be able to pick up on all of the signals that someone is sending, whether they be conscious or unconscious, apply the principles of framework analysis, and be able to read someone like a book within the first few minutes of meeting them.

That is the beauty of cold reading. And you will be able to do just that if you practice these skills as well. Just remember that this ability comes naturally with practice.

Now that we have a handle on what we will be covering in this guide, let's jump into the first part - the analysis frameworks.

Where the outer world is concerned, most people present an outer self that is curated, and reflective of our best qualities. We present ourselves in a way that is accepted by the groups we are in. The outer self is also related to how people cope with the demands of work and life, and may be concerned with practical day to day and materially focused things. If someone is not aware of their outer world, they may be criticized for sharing views that are contrary to popular opinion, or they may not be considerate of others. On the other hand, if one is too focused on their outer world, there may be a disconnect between what they are truly feeling, or their motivations behind their actions.

The inner world, in contrast, is all about what can't be seen from the outside. The inner world relates to feelings, intuition, true emotions, spirituality, desires, fantasies, and inner purpose and motivation. Someone who operates effectively in their inner world will have strong self-awareness as well as an understanding of their own beliefs, values and life purpose.

It is helpful to be aware, therefore, that the persona that someone portrays is not always completely in line with what they are experiencing on the inside.

If we want to become good at analyzing people, it is almost always required to interpret the behaviors and external actions of the persona, to remove the mask that they wear to get to the true thoughts and motivations of the individual.

We will use this concept as we dive further into behavioural analysis in this book. It is always helpful to keep in mind that when someone acts a certain way, it may be a coping or defense mechanism, or a pre-programmed behaviour that is there to hide one's true feelings, mask one's true intentions, or even deflect from criticism. Many of the strategies we will learn are focused on peeling back the onion of someone's psychology and revealing the true intentions that lie beyond the facade of their external behavior.

As we cover analysis systems in later chapters, always keep in mind how the concept of the Inner versus the Outer worlds may be coming into play and influencing the way we are interpreting and analyzing people's behavior.

When engaging in a conversation, we typically don't pay attention to the movements of the lower body. Since our direct line of sight is from the chest up, we often miss the obvious signs of the legs and feet. Certain stances that occur within the legs can signify dominance, sexual attraction, and even anxiety. Let's consider a few common patterns to look for when attempting to analyze someone else.

Crossed Legs

Crossed legs could indicate defensiveness. Perhaps you are sitting in a meeting at work, and your colleague says something totally off-putting. You may find yourself slowly crossing your legs as a subliminal way of showing your disapproval. Defensiveness could be heightened when one hand is positioned on top of the crossed leg. This is almost like a taunting move, signaling combat.

Crossing the ankles or knees are signs of nervousness, anxiety, and fear. This stance is protective in nature, which indicates that someone is attempting to protect themselves from whatever source of fear they are encountering. It could also be a means to control actions during high adrenaline situations.

Pointing and Active Legs

If you are miserable at a party, likely your legs are pointed towards the door as you are ready to leave. Our legs inadvertently point to where our heart wants to go. This can be used to determine interest and attraction. The legs, even when covered, will almost always point in the direction they are interested in.

Legs that bounce continuously could mean two things: boredom and nervousness. When you witness a person continuously bouncing their legs up and down, they may be nervous about something. This bounce is like a protective blanket that distracts their mind from their jitters. In addition, when someone is growing restless and ready to go, they may move their legs rapidly. The bouncing or tapping of the legs can be likened to a compulsion carried out to make the irritation subside.

When both legs point in one direction, it could be a clear indicator of interest for the person. However, when one leg steps back, it could indicate that the person wants distance. They may be uncomfortable with the person, conversation, or situation at hand. This subtle movement could be their way of escaping something distressful.

Messages from the Thighs

The upper portions of the legs usually indicate sexual or suggestive invitations between men and women. In daily activities, men may sit with their thighs opened as a sign of dominance. This outward display of masculinity represents an "alpha male" mentality. With women, closed thighs are a polite sign of femininity. Many young girls are instructed to sit with their legs closed so as not to expose their private areas. This closed manner of sitting is graceful and emanates class. When opened, they express dominance and even a form of female rebellion. Since it is so common for girls to be taught to keep their legs closed, doing the opposite could indicate opposition to societal norms. In addition, it is also extremely flirtatious to sit with the thighs crossed and one sitting higher above the other. This could indicate interest.

The Feet

The feet work very closely with the legs to determine areas of interest. When the toes are pointed at a specific object or direction, this indicates where we want to go. This could be a subtle signal your body sends to your mind about certain situations. The feet are used to make a statement and could also be used as an accent to verbal cues. Stomping, imaginative kicking, or tapping are all means of gaining attention.

When toddlers throw tantrums, it's not only their flailing arms, crying eyes, and yelling demands that occur. Toddlers utilize their legs and feet to create loud noises to further emphasize their anger.

When it comes to interpreting the signs of the legs and feet, direction and movement are the two primary components needed for translation. Although we typically fret from glancing at the bottom half of a person, simple movements could be a key indicator as to how a person is feeling. It's imperative to understand the beauty of intricate movements in order to fully understand the inner workings of another person.

CHAPTER 8

THE ART OF ANALYZING HUMAN BEHAVIOR.

As suggested, studying people is not reserved for psychiatrists but any other person even though psychiatrists are best positioned to analyze people. Analyzing people requires understanding their verbal and nonverbal cues. When studying people, you should try to remain objective and open to new information. Nearly each one of us has some form of personal biases and stereotypes that blocks our ability to understand another person correctly. When reading an individual, it is crucial to reconcile that information against the profession and cultural demands on the target person. Some environments may force an individual to exhibit particular behavior that is not necessarily part of their real one. For instance, working as a call center agent may force one to sound composed and patient when in real life, the person acts the contrary.

Start by analyzing the body language cues of the

target person you are trying to read. Body language provides the most authoritative emotional and physiological status of an individual. It is difficult to rehearse all forms of body language, and this makes body language critical in understanding a person. Verbal communication can be faked through rehearsal and experience, and this can give misleading stand. When examining body language, analyze the different types of body language as a set. For instance, analyze facial expressions, body posture, pitch, tonal variation, touch and eye contact, as a related but different manifestation of communication and emotional status. For instance, when tired, one is likely to stretch their arms and rest them on the left and right tops of adjacent chairs, sit in a slumped position, stare at the ceiling, and drop their heads. Analyzing only one aspect of body language can mislead one to come up with a conclusion correctly.

Additionally, it would be best if you lent attention to appearance. The first impression counts, but it can also be misleading. In formal contexts, the appearance of an individual is critical to communicate the professionalism of the person and the organizational state of the mind of that individual. For example, an individual with an unbuttoned shirt indicates he hurried or is casual with the audience and the message. Wearing formal attire that is buttoned and tucked in suggests prior preparation and seriousness that the person lends to the occasion. Having unkempt hair may indicate a rebellious mind, and this might be common among African professors in Africa, for instance. In most settings, having unkempt hair suggests that one lacks the discipline to prepare for the formal context or the person is overworked and is busy. Lack of expected grooming may indicate an individual battling with life challenges or feeling uncared for.

It is also important that one should take note of the posture of the person. Posture communicates a lot about the involvement of an individual in a conversation. Having an upright posture suggests eagerness and active participation in what is being communicated. If one cups their face in the arms and lets the face rest on both thighs, then it suggests that one is feeling exhausted or has deviated from the conversation completely. Having crossed arms suggests defensiveness or deep thought. One sitting in a slumped position suggests that he/she is tired and not participating in the ongoing conversation. Leaning on the wall or any object suggests casualness that the person is lending to an ongoing conversation. If at home, sitting with crossed legs suggests that one is completely relaxed. However, the same posture at the workplace suggests that one is feeling tensed and at the same time concentrating.

Furthermore, observe the physical movements in terms of distance and gestures. The distance between you and the target individual is communicating communicates about the level of respect and assurance that the individual perceives. A social distance is the safest bet when communicating, and it suggests high levels of professionalism or respect between the participants. Human beings tend to be territorial as exhibited by the manner that they guard their distance. Any invasion of the personal distance will make the individual defensive and unease with the interaction.

For this reason, when an individual shows discomfort when the distance between communicators is regarded as social or public, then the individual may have other issues bothering him or her. Social and public distances should make one feel fully comfortable.

Allowing a person close enough or into the personal distance suggests that the individual feels secure and familiar with the other person. Through reading, the distance between the communicators will give a hint on the respect, security, and familiarity between the individuals as well the likely profession of the individuals.

Correspondingly, then try to read facial expressions as deep frown lines indicate worry or over-thinking. Facial expressions are among the visible and critical forms of body language and tell more about the true emotional status of an individual. For instance, twitching the mouth suggests that an individual is not listening and is showing disdain to the speaker. A frozen face indicates that the person is shell-shocked, and this can happen when making a presentation of health and diseases or when releasing results of an examination. A smiling face with the smile not being prolonged communicates that one is happy and following the conversation. A prolonged smile suggests sarcasm. If one continually licks, the lips may indicate that one is lying or that one is feeling disconnected from the conversation.

Relatedly, try to create a baseline for what merits as

normal behavior. As you will discover, people have distinct mannerisms that may be misleading to analyze them as part of the communication process. For instance, some individuals will start a conversation by looking down or at the wall before turning to the audience. Mildly, mannerisms are like a ritual that one must activate before they make a delivery. Additionally, each person uniquely expresses the possible spectra of body language. By establishing a baseline of what is normal behavior, one gets to identify and analyze deviations from the standardized normal behavior accurately. Against this understanding, one will not erratically score a speaker that shuffles first if that is part of his behavior when speaking to an audience.

Furthermore, pay attention to inconsistencies between the established baseline that you have created and the individual's gestures and words. Once you have created a baseline, then examine for any deviations from this baseline. For instance, if one speaks in a high-pitched voice that is uncharacteristically of the individual, then the person may be feeling irritated. If one normally walks across the stage when speaking but the individual chooses to speak from a fixed position during the current speech, then the person is exhibiting a deviation that may suggest that the individual is having self-awareness or is feeling unease with the current audience. If an individual speaks fast, but usually the person speaks with a natural flow, then the person is in a hurry or has not prepared for the task.

Correspondingly, view gestures as clusters to elicit a meaning of what the person is communicating or trying to hide. When speaking a person, will express different gestures and dwelling on the current gesture may make you arrive at a misleading conclusion. Instead, one should view the gestures as clusters and interpret what they imply. For instance, if a speaker throws the hands randomly in the air, raises one of their feet, stamps the floor and shakes his or her hands, then all of these could suggest a speaker that is feeling irked and disappointed by the audience or the message. As such, different aspects of body language should be interpreted as a unit rather than in isolation.

Then compare and contrast. For one to fully read the target person, try comparing the body language of the person against the entire group or audience. For instance, if one appears bored and other people appear bored, then you should conclude the tiredness of the person is largely due to the actions of the speaker for speaking longer than necessary. In other terms, the body language of the target person is not isolated. However, if you make a comparison, and it happens that the target person's body language deviated from the rest, then you should profile the actions of the individual accordingly. Making a comparison and contrast helps arrive at a fair judgment of the target person.

By the same measure, try to make the individual react to your intentional communication. Another way of managing to read a person is to initiate communication and watch their reaction. For instance, establishing eye contact and evaluating the reciprocation of the target person can help tell more about their confidence and activeness in participating in the interaction. When an individual ignores your attempts to initiate communication, the person could be concentrating on other things, or the person feels insecure. Initiating communication is critical where it is difficult to profile a person, and one wants to convincingly read the person.

Go further and try to identify the strong voice. A

strong voice suggests the confidence and authority of the speaker. If the speaker lacks a strong voice, then he or she is new to what is being presented or has stage fright. However, having a strong voice that is not natural suggests a spirited attempt to appear in charge and confident. A strong voice should be natural if the individual is feeling composed and confident in what he or she is talking about.

Relatedly, observe how the individual walks. When speaking to a target person, he or she will walk across the stage or make movements around the site where the conversation is happening. From the manner of walking, we can read a lot about the individual. Frequently walking up and down while speaking to an audience may indicate panic or spirited attempt to appear in control. Speaking while walking slowly across the stage from one end to the other end indicates that one is comfortable speaking to the audience. If a member of the audience poses a question, and one walks towards the individual, then it suggests interest in clarifying what the individual is asking.

It might be necessary to scout for personality cues. Fortunately, all people have identifiable personalities, but these can be difficult to read for a person not trained in a psychologist. However, through observation, one will get cues on the personality of the individual. For instance, an outgoing person is likely to show a warm smile and laugh at jokes. A socially warm person is likely to want to make personal connections when speaking, such as mentioning a particular person in the audience. Reserved individuals are likely to use fewer words in their communication and appear scared or frozen on stage when speaking.

Additionally, one should listen to intuition, as it is often valid. Gut feelings are often correct, and when reading a person, you should give credence to your gut feeling about the person. When reading a person and you get a feeling that the person is socially warm, you should entertain this profiling while analyzing the body language of the person. While considering gut feeling, you should classify it under subjective analysis, as it is not based on observable traits and behaviors but an inner feeling.

Expectedly, watch the eye contact. Creating eye contact suggests eagerness and confidence in engaging the audience. Avoiding eye contact suggests stage fright and shyness as well as lack confidence in what one is talking about. A sustained look is a stare, and it is intended to intimidate, or it may suggest absentmindedness of the individual. If one continuously blinks eyes while looking at a target person suggests a flirting behavior. An eye contact that gradually drops to the chest and thigh of the individual suggests a deviation of thoughts from the conversation.

Additionally, pay attention to touch. The way a person shakes hands speaks a lot about their confidence and formality. A firm handshake that is brief indicates confidence and professionalism. A weak handshake that is brief indicates that one is feeling unease. On the other hand, a prolonged handshake, whether weak or strong, suggests that the person is trying to flirt with you, especially if it is between opposite sexes. Touching someone on the head may suggest rudeness and should be avoided.

Finally, listen to the tone of voice and laughter. Laughing may suggest happiness or sarcasm. Americans are good at manifesting sarcastic laughter, and it is attained by varying the tones of the laughter. The tone of the voice tells if the person is feeling confident and authoritative or not. Overall, a tonal variation implies that the individual is speaking naturally and convincingly. A flat tone indicates a lack of self-confidence and unfamiliarity with the conversation or audience and should be avoided.

Distance in Communication

If one is talking to someone, the person violates your personal space, and you allow it, then it signals that you are okay to intimate ideas. Intimate ideas in this context include highly personal issues that one can talk with another person. For instance, if you walk and sit close and in contact with a woman watching television and she approves your behavior, then it is indicative that she is likely to allow you have a personal talk that may be intimate in nature. Such discussion may include your health challenges or mental health and not necessarily sexual issues. For this reason, one should carefully weigh the need to invade the personal distance.

Regarding children, violating personal distance will make them freeze due to feeling uncomfortable. If a teacher sits next to a student or stands next to a student, then the student is likely to feel uneasy and nervous. However, they are instances where the invasion of personal space is allowed and seen as necessary. For instance, during interviews or when being examined by a doctor, invasion of private space by the person with advantage is allowed. The panel during an interview may move or ask you to move closer, which may violate your personal space. A doctor may also stand closer to you, invading your personal space, but this is necessary due to the professional demand of their service.

As such, when one avoids personal distance, and the individual is expected to be within this space, then the individual may be feeling less confident or feeling ashamed. For instance, if a child has done something embarrassing, he or she is likely to sit or stand far from the parent during a conversation. For this reason, it appears that one should feel confident, assured, and appreciated to approach and remain in personal space when needed.

Additionally, staying in personal space during intense emotions may portray one as resilient, understanding, and bold. Think of two lovers or sibling quarreling, but each remains in the established personal space. The message that is being communicated is that the individual is confident that he or she can handle the intense emotions from the other person. For most people, they only allow their lover to stay in their personal distance when feeling upset because they trust that the person can handle the known behavior of the affected person. Since being in personal space places a person within physical striking range, most people will only allow trusted and familiar individuals into their personal space.

Equally important is that invasion of personal space is justified because it is part of professional demands. Think of a new teacher that is trying to help a student solve a mathematical equation. In this aspect, the teacher is a stranger because he or she is new to the school. By sitting or standing close to, the student, the teacher is invading the personal space, but the established norms in this context allow the student not to feel unease. For emphasis, this case is not unique as it aligns with stated expectations that people will welcome known or unfamiliar people in their personal space only if they trust them and, in this case, the student feels safe with any teacher. For this reason, the operationalization of distance in communication is mediated and moderated by established culture.

In most cases, one can start with public distance

before allowing the interaction to happen in personal or social space. For instance, as a student during tournaments, you could have initiated nonverbal communication with the student from the other college before suddenly feeling connected to the individual and allowing him or her to move into personal space as a potential girlfriend or boyfriend. At first, the target person saw you as a stranger but allowed you to make nonverbal communication within the public space. When the person felt the need to connect more with you and have given you the benefit of the doubt, the person allowed you to move through public distance and social distance to enter their personal space.

For instance, a lot can be learned from studying distance and space in communication. Being allowed into the social and personal distances implies that the person trusts that you will not harm them emotionally and physically. For the intimate distance, being allowed into this distance implies that the person trusts you so much and is confident that you can never harm them and that you share a lot. For instance, a mother holding her baby close enough to her signals that the baby is feeling assured of security and protection. When two lovers move, closer until their faces are almost touching suggests trust and confidence that the other person feels safe and protected.

Relatedly, if arguing with your child or lover and the individual moves farther from you physically, then it suggests that the person no longer feels safe with you being within their personal distance. Issues that can cause someone to expand the distance between you and them include the risk of violence from you and emotional issues. If you occasionally act violently, then chances are, your lover or children will expand the personal distance to social distance because this is where they feel safe due to your personality and character. It then appears that your prior behavior will also affect the distance during communication.

Nevertheless, they are other issues that cause individuals to extend the distance of interaction, and these include having a medical condition or having hygiene issues. For instance, if you are sweaty, then chances are that the other person may prefer to extend the distance of communication between you and them. Having oral hygiene issues may also make the other person move far away from you because the smell turns them off. For this reason, interpreting the distance between communicators should also include hygiene and health-related issues that impact this distance.

For instance, some medical conditions can make people maintain some distance from you or be closer to you physically. For instance, some conditions may attract uneasiness, and this includes epilepsy. People with epilepsy get seizures, and this can make people feel unease being closer to them because they inadvertently fall. On the other hand, having hearing issues or sore throat may make people move closer to you physically to facilitate effective communication. However, these are exceptions when analyzing space and distance as forms of nonverbal communication, but they should be taken into account where necessary.

In some cases, it is welcome to invade personal distance merely by circumstances. For instance, when attending a match in a full packed stadium or sitting to watch a movie in a movie theater, one will have his personal invaded due to the sitting arrangements. In this context, one may feel uneasy with this arrangement, but he or she has little control of the situation. While we value and seek to protect personal spaces, some situations make us allowing invasion of this space because it is beyond control.

Activity

1. Mark is talking to his girlfriend, and their noses are almost touching. Comment on what this means. Do you feel that the actions of Mark are appropriate? Why or Why not?

2. The following day, Mark is talking to his girlfriend while standing nine feet away. Comment on what this means.

3. An elderly person asks Mark to assist him in how to shop online using the smartphone. Richard is standing right next to this elderly person. Comment on what this means.

4. On Saturday, Mark argued with his sister. He was visibly angry, but they continued exchanging words while seated on the same sofa set. Comment on this distance and space in communication. Comment on the importance of trust and assurance for people who share this space.

5. Mark met his girlfriend while attending a football match. It all started when Mark threw a hard stare at her at the farthest end of the stand.

When the girl reciprocated the stare, Mark moved closer to her after the game and they walked holding hands. This is an example of allowing someone to transit from public distance to personal distance. Using analysis of distance and space in communication only, why do you think the girl allowed Mark to shorten the distance and welcome him into the personal space?

6. Nicole works as a nurse at the local clinic. When one of the patients asked for a nurse, Nicole moved close enough to the patient and touched his hand to examine it. What is the justification for this distance in this communication?

7. Nicole and her husband quarreled last night, and today they sat eight feet from each other while pretending nothing happened. Using the concept of space and distance only, suggest two reasons for this behavior?

8. As a new mother, Nicole holds her baby closer, making her nose and that of the baby touch while making sounds to the baby. Justify why this distance and space in communication is allowed?

9. Last month while seated on a bench in a public park, a stranger walked and sat right next to Nicole even though the bench had only Nicole. Nicole decided to stand up and walk away. Why do you think Nicole walked away? Use only the concept of distance and space to explain.

Major Components to Connectivity

There exist three critical components that determine a person's ability to connect with others successfully. They are; mindful observation, listening with intent, and useful feedback.

Linking with Other People Through Mindful Observation

What is a mindful remark? Just like most of us, you observe people and your surroundings at all the time, but what happens to other things apart from the stuff you discovered? How to apply what you have discovered to support your screening and adapt your behaviors and objectives? Normally, most people work with incredibly little of what they find to boost their calls. If they ever happen to be over-informed, they might find out what happens in declaring what normally does not sit well with the crowd. As a result, they quit conversing. Many people are essential in the making of extremely few modifications to increase their marketing and sales communications. Instead, they dialogue with a person who is definitely excited to participate.

In most cases, there is lack of monitoring and adjustment of verbal and non-verbal terminologies because many individuals never learned the skills on how to analyze people and they change their communication style to be very accommodating to match a person's personality. Remark forces help people to place what they discover to function and generate a livelier exchange of details.

To improve your remarks expertise, ensure to tackle the job like a pup! You heard that right, just like a pup. Pet dogs exhibit amazing interest in watching expertise. This simply means that dog trainers declare the very best approach to show a pup how to carry out the strategy by enabling them to see another puppy perform it and receive a prize. A dog's remark abilities will be excited that they ought to study better through observation, rather than spoken instructions. Who says that the same procedure is not applicable to humans?

Marsha's puppy is very observant; Hannah knows what she will be doing a time structured schedule in the items as she observes her own activity. For instance, if Marsha draws out her operating shoes or boots, Hannah is aware they will be heading to work. If Marsha holds her hair back into a ponytail, Hannah will suspect they will be going herding and working into the storage units. This means hanging on to a car door because Marsha definitely wears her mane in a ponytail when she and Hannah are herding.

The problem is that when Marsha decides to pull her hair into a ponytail, and she's not taking Hannah herding. Usually, Hannah is sure she's heading out to the herd, and she will commence to scratch and pester Marsha about why the turn was dragged. Hannah is very unremitting in her efforts to get Marsha to carry out what she needs as they might commence in the near future. Therefore, Hannah is sure of her potential in analyzing her owner and knowing that she will be standing at the storage door for almost an hour waiting for Marsha's method. Although Hannah reads all the signals, she failed to understand that the same signal could possess countless definitions.

The moral of the story is to caution you that

sometimes you can have excellent observation skills with this particular person. What you observe and affix a meaning is not a preference of what was expected. You can carry out the same issues; however, you lack the desired tools. Your connection does not get better; neither can your relationship. When this occurs, it implies there are modification issues. Stop supposing that the same analysis will apply to everyone. Make efforts for something leading to acquiring better sales and marketing communications. The crucial aspect to remember is that giving up will get you nowhere.

Sometimes you need to observe a little or a bit longer. Don't just look at the person as they communicate with you; watch their communication cues with others. Watch how others react to them. If the person with whom you are having issues and watching their body language is around the individuals they like, make efforts to pay attention to their tone as they speak with other people with whom they talk to in a pleasant way. Simply observe how various people respond to a person with whom you have problems with. How is their tone? What is their body language expressing? How will the ranking be? For confusing interactions, surface area findings are not necessarily enough.

Be mindful of your goals when observing your subject. What do you want from the relationship? Being aware means you can't always be focusing on all the things going on around others, but you need to choose one or two things to observe for some time until when you have a greater understanding of what they are saying with their gestures or expressions. After knowing what their moves will be on something else, you need to be mindful with the observation means with which you are determined to resolve the situation and improve the communication with that person.

Hearing with Intent

People observe others every moment; they listen to what they say very well. The disadvantage is that you can notice an individual, but if you are tuning in with a particular motive, you will not know what to do with what you have discovered. For example, you can hear an individual speak, but if you are not able to distinguish the person's dialogue level when they are conversing or the quantity in which they speak with a system in the discovery of their personality type, you hear a portion of the subject matter.

When playing with intent, you might have the

tendency of interrupting. This tendency system shows where you are heading to after the difference in communication shows that you have a tendency of speaking more than the person. In fact, you have a tendency to speak a lot; you are attentive to the motive of sense, which implies behind the phrases and between the lines.

Providing an Actual Opinion

There are times when providing effective opinions is a way of mimicking a person's price or quantity of conversation. Sometimes, useful opinions will mean implementing a relaxed open stance to reveal what you like to observe the other person do. There are occasions when useful opinions will mean modifying your personality characteristics so that you can avoid making the other person uncomfortable or angry. If your concept is garbled due to your body vocabulary, gestures, and expressions diverging from your words, you ought to provide clarity to the discussion by giving congruent opinions.

In a program, there are occasions where you avoid creating avenues for people to read your thoughts. Therefore, effective opinions will be those masking the way one experiences. It is not about hiding your thoughts, but handling them. It is not about how effective you or anyone else seem, but how you generally show every sole assumption and sensing. There are situations when you want to bury your thoughts a little bit to ensure devices don't present you or set you in any insecure opportunities. In such a circumstance, powerful remarks do NOT unveil what you never wish another to discover.

Practicing these three major factors for connectivity, and other folks might be linked to you. Nevertheless, they might give more support to your thoughts and ideas. It is an approach to acquiring what you wish without mental outbursts and unreasonable requirements. You can maintain your approach since you are a remarkable communicator. You acquire the support from others since they like you; with this, you can quickly get to them. You can attain achievements in your personal and professional lifestyle because you hook up with others and they with you, this include all the results of the few approaches you have discovered from these web pages. Do you have an apparent tendency? Then you've just used the three critical elements to connectivity: mindful statement, listening with intention, and providing useful opinions.

Word Clues You Need to Know

"I Labored Hard to Accomplish My Dreams"

The clue in this sentence is labored hard, and it shows that the person's dreams were difficult to accomplish. Perhaps it took him longer and harder to accomplish this particular dream as compared to the other goals he has accomplished. When we delve deeper, you will discover that the word clue labored suggests the person holds the belief that dedication and hard work can produce great result.

"I Bagged Another Contract"

The word clue is another, and it reveals that the speaker or writer has won so many contracts and this is just the latest accomplishment. From the above sentence, you can deduce that the speaker wants everyone who cared to listen to know that he won so many awards. He is trying to bolster his self-image by appearing successful. To an astute observer, this person seems self-conscious about what others think. More so, he needs the adulation of others to boost his self-esteem. Others who noticed this character weakness might try to exploit it for their personal gains.

"Jim and I Remained Friends"

The word clue in this sentence is remained. From the sentence, you can deduce that the speaker and Jim have gone through trying times. Perhaps the fabric of their friendship has gone through different difficult situations. They probably weren't supposed to be friends under normal circumstances. The speaker is trying to defend why she remained friend with Jim. The speaker doesn't feel convinced about her choice and, therefore, feels the need to defend her decision.

"I Patiently Sat through the Meeting"

Here, the word clue patiently holds a plethora of hypotheses. For instance, the speaker might be bored with the lecture but felt obligated to sit through it for various reasons. Perhaps the speaker had to use the restroom but felt self-conscious or trapped from standing up to go the restroom. You could also deduce from the statement that she might have had an urgent appointment somewhere else.

Gauging from this statement, we can accurately say the speaker is someone who adheres to social etiquette and norms, irrespective of other pressing needs. Those with no social boundaries would have left the lecture to attend to any other issue that needs their attention. People with social boundaries like the speaker would make good employees since they know how to follow the rules and respect authority.

Conversely, those who leave during the lecture to attend to other pressing needs are perfect candidates for jobs that require out-of-the-box thinking.

"I Decided to Buy That Dress"

The modifier or world clue here is decided. It indicates that the speaker weighed several options before settling for that particular dress. This statement shows us that the speaker is not impulsive. Rather, she weighs her options and takes the most logical step. More so, there's a high chance our speaker is an introvert since introverts tend to weigh their options before taking a step.

It's not a sure analysis, but a hypothesis about the speaker's personality. Conversely, an impulsive person would say, "I just bought that dress." The word clue just represents an impulsive decision.

"I Did the Right Thing"

The word clue, 'right', suggests that the speaker

struggled with a moral or ethical dilemma before arriving at the decision. This verbal statement suggests that the person has a solid strength of character to make the best and just decision in the face of overwhelming opposing views.

CONCLUSION

The body is a fascinating group of systems that work coherently to expose our innermost emotions. From a simple glimpse of the eyes all the way down to the positioning of the toes, the body is honest. Mastering the art of analyzing others begins with a comprehensive understanding of yourself. Even different inflections of the voice can change a sentence in its entirety. In addition, the art of touch can mean the difference between attraction and repulsion. Learning how to analyze others assists with social connection and your ability to understand what others are truly saying. The beauty behind the human connection is that there are universal mannerisms that give off social cues open for interpretation. A simple shrug of the brows paired with a crossing of the arms signals a sign of discontent. A slight lean inward can give you the signal that your date is legitimately into you! These subtle cues are intricate in nature, but the magnitude is revolutionary. By mastering these techniques, you will have this unwavering gift that is easily applicable to your everyday life. You will be able to seek the truth and defend yourself against possible threats. One of the key secrets to mastering the art of analyzing others is keying in on your observation skills. The entire body works in conjunction with the brain to send and expel certain messages that define emotions, often leading to subconscious visual cues that may give away the true thoughts and feelings of a given individual without their even realizing what they are doing. Inside, you will find dozens of different ways to pick up on those cues for fun and profit. By being observant and truly reading the behaviors of others, you will be able to emphasize this gift to meet your needs. We encourage you to implement these practices into your daily life to further analyze yourself and truly be able to read others.

The next step is to practice these tips throughout your daily life! By doing so, you will gain a better understanding of yourself and human behavior as a whole.

www.ingramcontent.com/pod-product-compliance
Lightning Source LLC
Chambersburg PA
CBHW060311030426
42336CB00011B/1002